WINNING FAITH

THE MARGARET COURT STORY

WITH
BARBARA OLDFIELD

Strand Publishing
Sydney

CONTENTS

ACKNOWLEDGMENTS

I would like to thank the following people for making the reprint of *Winning Faith* possible:

Barbara Oldfield, one of my dear friends, who wrote the original manuscript and contributed greatly to this revised edition.
David Dixon, publisher, who has coordinated and overseen this revised edition superbly.
Owen Salter, editor, whose editing and diligent research skills have ensured an honest account of my life and ministry over the past eight years.
Jackie Battley, my secretary, who again helped with proofreading.

I pray that you are blessed by the words on the following pages and that they come alive in you. Allow God to make the difference in your life, spirit, soul and body. He is no respecter of persons; what He has done for me, He will do for you.

Margaret Court

CHAMPIONSHIP RECORD*

Australian Open
Singles: 1960–66; 1969–71; 1973
Doubles: 1961–63; 1965; 1969–71; 1973
Mixed Doubles: 1963–1965; 1969**

Wimbledon Championships
Singles: 1963; 1965; 1970
Doubles: 1964; 1969
Mixed Doubles: 1963; 1965–66; 1968; 1975

United States Open
Singles: 1962; 1965; 1969–70; 1973
Doubles: 1963; 1968; 1970; 1973; 1975
Mixed Doubles: 1961–65; 1969; 1970; 1972

French Open
Singles: 1962; 1964; 1969–70; 1973
Doubles: 1964–66; 1973
Mixed Doubles: 1963–65; 1969

Italian Championship
Singles: 1962–64
Doubles: 1963–64; 1968
Mixed Doubles: 1961; 1964; 1968

South African Open
Singles: 1968; 1970–71
Doubles: 1966; 1971
Mixed Doubles: 1966; 1970–71; 1974

German Open
Singles: 1964; 1965; 1966
Doubles: 1964; 1965; 1966
Mixed Doubles: 1965; 1966

Federation Cup
The International Teams Championship
1963–65; 1968–69; 1971 (Margaret won every singles match she played—20 out of 20.)

* Source: International Tennis Federation
** Many sources credit Margaret Court with sixty-two Grand Slam titles, because they exclude her 'divided wins' in the Australian Open mixed doubles in 1965 and 1969.

INTRODUCTION

S port provides tremendous entertainment. There is something intrinsically exciting about watching battles of immense proportions being fought out, with only one of the two combatants—either an individual or a team—being declared the winner. I for one always enjoyed winning; it was just the rarity of the wins that spoiled that particular enjoyment! But that could not be said of Margaret Court, who also enjoyed winning. For her it was losses that were a rarity!

Although I was headed for the top in squash, being the fifth ranked player in the world in 1982 before I was forced to retire through illness, I never quite made it to the winners' circle as often as she did. But there were very few players in the world in any sport who collected as many trophies as she did. Her incredible record of sixty-four Grand Slam titles is almost unbelievable, but the records faithfully document each one of those amazing victories.

I made one of my biggest mistakes when I first started writing this book ten years ago: I invited the 'Queen of Wimbledon' to play a fun game of squash with me as a battle of the 'oldies'. It became very apparent even in the hit up that she was not used to having her opponent on the same side of the court, for the arc of her swing could cut a path from Perth to Sydney. Secondly, the back wall was not really a consideration for her as she preferred to forget any ball that slipped past her amazing reach. Her whole intent was to dominate the central court area and put into effect her cut-off volley.

The years had done nothing to diminish her tenacity and determination. We could have been playing for the championship of the world as she ran for what I thought were 'impossible' shots and even tried to volley away my drop-shot winners. I had always thought of myself as the most competitive person I knew, but watching Margaret made me think again.

It was not hard to see why she had won so many titles. She didn't know the meaning of the word 'quit'. Any ball that came anywhere near her was punched back into play with an awesome power generated by her lethal swing. It was the balls she reached for just over my head that worried me the most: I exercised far more that day than I had expected to, skilfully dodging her swing to avoid having my head neatly removed. *I hope her faith is high*, I thought. *She may have to use it to raise me from the dead if one of those full-bodied swings connects!*

I am happy to report that I emerged that day with a narrow win and life and limb intact. That Margaret had also become the second ranked squash player in Western Australia during her 1966 retirement did not surprise me one bit.

Besides our common interest in sport, Margaret and I share a great spiritual affinity. It was in the family room of her home in 1980 that I gave my life to Christ. It was a wonderful day as the sun's rays cascaded playfully into the room creating a spectacular effect. Like most people, I had experienced emotional and physical traumas of some magnitude before I realised that I could not make it on my own. These were the catalysts that pushed me to my knees—a great position to pray.

Within two months the immediate traumas had passed, so I took myself back again into the world, the flesh and the devil. For a while Jesus had been my crutch, but now that I was well again I had no intentions of 'going religious'—a prospect that excited me about as much as being ravaged by a dead sheep. It was unfortunate for me that I didn't go further and make Jesus my wheelchair, because although I couldn't see it at the time, I was once again on the path to ruin.

The best description I can give of my existence over the next ten years is 'life on a roller-coaster'—sometimes up and sometimes down, it all depended on the circumstances. Winning made me happy, losing did not. This applied to sport and to my life in general.

But through all these turbulent years Margaret was always there for me. She never criticised me or condemned me in any way for my many failings. It was as though she knew I would have to run the race my way (the theme song of the journey to hell could well be 'I Did It My Way'). And my life really was like hell; it certainly wasn't anything like heaven.

Finally the realisation that I had run *from* God

instead of *to* Him came as I saw God's love at work in Margaret. It was her unchangeable advice (always straight from God's Word), her unconditional love and acceptance, and her refusal to give up on me, knowing that the day would come when I would come home to God as His long lost 'prodigal son'.

Today I have come full circle. I no longer live in the fear and uncertainty of the world; I live in the faith and certainty of God. Since I made such a mess of it my way, it was obvious that His way was the only way to go if I was to enjoy success in every dimension of my life.

I became a part of Margaret Court Ministries Inc. in 1991 because I have the same heart desire that Margaret has to see all the lost, lonely and hurting people in the world come to know Christ, the only real source of strength and comfort in these turbulent times.

Our battle today is not being fought in the sporting arenas of the world but on the streets of Perth, where we fight against the forces of darkness that keep people's eyes blinded to their need for a Saviour. Victory in winning souls is always sweet. There is unspeakable joy in being a champion for God.

The story I tell in the following pages is one of victory and defeat, for while Margaret was a winner in tennis she was not necessarily a winner in life. Her story will encourage you when you find yourself reflected in her experiences of fear, guilt and worthlessness, all of which she finally overcame. If you apply the same principles, you too will be able to overcome any areas of defeat in your own life.

At the back of the book is a small prayer that you may want to pray when you've finished reading. If you are the only person who prays this prayer out of a conviction gained from reading *Winning Faith*, then I feel I will have told the story well.

Barbara Oldfield

Chapter 1

A Ball, a Plank and a Garage Wall

Margaret Smith Court is without doubt the most successful tennis player of all time, amassing sixty-four Grand Slam titles. She won eleven Australian Opens, five US Opens, five French Opens and three Wimbledon Opens in singles, nineteen doubles, and a further twenty-one mixed doubles. If that was not enough, she also won twenty-six Italian, German and South African Opens in both singles and doubles.

She was only a teenager of seventeen when she began on the senior circuit in 1960 and was still playing fourteen years later, taking three Grand Slam titles in 1973, a remarkable achievement considering she had taken two years out. She had an amazing ability to come back from retirement and childbirth to fulfil her goals when many others would simply have quit.

She never knew how to quit right from the time of her birth in 1942—a time of war and great fear in Australia, for it seemed inevitable that the Japanese would invade the country's northern shores. But in

Albury, New South Wales, Maude Smith's greatest concern was not the war but whether she would safely deliver her fourth child in life-threatening circumstances. The battle was won, and both she and her new daughter, named Margaret, went proudly home after the 'miracle' birth.

Margaret grew up with her mother being very fearful. The thought of nearly losing Margaret at birth made her all the more determined that nothing would harm or injure her youngest child. Not that she wasn't as protective of all her children—her fear of strange people and places was so intense it bordered on paranoia.

Unfortunately for Mrs Smith, Margaret developed at an alarming rate. She crawled, walked and climbed at an age when other babies were content to lie there and be entertained. Her toddler years were a nightmare for her fearful mother, and her pre-school years were no better. Mrs Smith often thought she had given birth to another son as Margaret lived life at such a pace that she out-played and out-ran every other child, male or female, in the district.

The country lifestyle of Albury suited her long-legged athletic disposition. She much preferred to be outdoors running, jumping, kicking or hitting a ball than inside playing with dolls!

All through primary school she felt she was wasting precious time. It took a real effort for her to sit for long hours in the classroom. For her, the schoolroom paled into insignificance compared to the 'outdoor' schoolroom where she learnt so much from her broad and vast hands-on experiences.

She loved nothing better than to hear the old school bell toll the close of day. By the time she was in the fifth grade, all she wanted to do was to go out and hit a tennis ball against any convenient wall, hour after hour, using any apparatus that resembled a tennis racquet.

She lived for the weekends when there was no school. Her favourite pastime was to go fishing with her Dad along the banks of the beautiful Murray River. Large cod would often grace their dinner table after their successful trips. The Murray was her Mississippi and she, its Huckleberry Finn. This river was endless in its possibilities. She would hide in its tangled old logs and the gnarled reeds along its banks, drop from old tyres hanging from the trees into its cool waters during the oppressive heat of a summer's day, and fish its precious contents right out onto a plate.

Margaret had no real girlfriends. She was the leader, by virtue of her greater height, over a small gang of boys on whom she constantly practised her leadership abilities. She was their Boadicea, bold and daring. Girls never acted like she did—she was just one of the guys!

The Smith family was not wealthy but there was an abundance of activity in their family home. Her Dad was the foreman in the local ice-cream factory, and her popularity rose markedly on Saturdays when the free ice-creams came home with him.

But her mother was a champion worrier. She worried incessantly about every conceivable thing; and if by mistake there was nothing to worry about, she worried that she wasn't worried about something, for something bad was obviously just around the corner waiting to happen.

She was never at peace with her family and always feared the worst in every situation. The family would take hours to persuade her just to go for a drive with them, but when she did she insisted that they take her straight home because she had left the stove on. Invariably she had not, but despite assurances to the contrary, Mrs Smith could not relax until she went home to see. Fear gripped her life, and imaginations in every dimension played havoc with her mind, developing into severe phobias.

Lawrence, Margaret's father, was quite the opposite. He had a zest for life and loved nothing more than taking his youngest daughter fishing. He really didn't worry about much at all! Margaret was caught somewhere in the middle, learning to worry like her mother and also hearing how to relax and have fun without a care like her father.

The gang under her control often played tricks which would have given Mrs Smith good reason to worry had she known about them.

A curve in the highway, just on the outskirts of town, was a braking point for the road trains before they came into town. It was also lined with large bushes in which the gang could hide out and wait for a driver to slow down his truck. Once they heard the lowering of the gears, they would quickly climb aboard the tailgates of the now slow-moving road train to catch a ride to the next turn in the road. Daringly foolhardy, they held on like riders on a rodeo horse, ready to jump off just before they entered the turn.

Then laughing and with the adrenalin pumping freely, they trotted back to do it all again.

At times they would take with them a large brown paper parcel, and, to break the monotony of the afternoon waiting for 'free rides', they would tie the parcel with string and throw it into the middle of the road. Like fishermen perched on rocks, they hid patiently in the bushes waiting for a bite, the parcel being the bait. As speeding motorists approached, they often went past the parcel only to back up to see what it was. Of course, once they started backing up, the parcel mysteriously disappeared into the safety of the bushes with a hefty tug on the string. Outright laughter had to be suppressed to avoid detection by the bemused motorists, who stood scratching their heads in bewilderment.

On one occasion a humourless fellow saw the parcel disappear into the bushes and went in after it. The gang fled in all directions, their fleet-footedness assuring their escape from the cursing, lumbering figure. They met as usual by the local river and daringly dropped into the water from the overhanging tree branches, then lay like sprawled out crabs in the sun to dry their clothes before going home for tea.

By the time she was eight Margaret had taken to 'tennis', which meant hitting a hairless ball with a plank of wood against the garage wall. She recognised quickly she would need some hitting companions to make it more enjoyable and to fetch the odd ball or two. So half the gang were ordered to volunteer their time to hit balls with her on the road outside her home. Right across the road from her house were the twenty-four grass courts of the Albury Tennis Club, but they were for members only.

However, not being members was not about to stop this gang. Once Margaret felt her standard of play had progressed satisfactorily, she led them onto the back court through a hole in the hedge. Previous reconnaissance had shown that three-quarters of this court were totally hidden from the club house by a magnificently located cypress tree; only the back quarter was exposed. Here they could play to their hearts' content as long as the ball didn't go to the back of the court. So on their first visit Margaret decided that she, being head and shoulders over the rest of them, should station herself at the net to stop the balls going through to the back. This, of course, meant she had to try to volley anything that came her way. Without knowing it, she had begun to practise the very stroke that would mark her future dominance of women's tennis.

But on this very first day and on this big occasion she was anything but dominant, and their two balls repeatedly went over her head to the back of the court, despite her urgings to the three boys on the other side of the net to keep them down.

Each took a turn at retrieving the balls by crawling on their stomachs to the back of the court, keeping their heads well down all the time and hoping the local professional, Mr Rutter, wasn't at that moment fixing his eye on the outer court. Unfortunately for them, he had already spied the 'illegal immigrants' and was on his way to clear them off his beloved grass, every blade of which he treated with the same respect certain women have for their sons.

One look at them, with not a sandshoe or anything that resembled white clothing between them, left him open-mouthed. Their racquets were more like lethal weapons or relics from a lost age, with the misshapen look that comes from being left all day in the sun and overnight in the rain.

'Clear off, you young rascals!' he ordered in a gruff way. And scamper they did, in record time, exiting through the same hole that had been their entrance, trailing their array of racquets with them. They knew— and he did too—that there would be another day. The fear of detection made it all the more exciting!

Mr Rutter appeared to be tough, but they noticed that he never once plugged the hole in the hedge. The gang were often unofficially on his courts.

Not long afterwards, Wal Rutter began Saturday morning clinics for the juniors in the district. If the interest of Margaret and her gang was anything to go by, he felt the kids must be keen and ready for some type of formal tennis instruction. Indeed they were— and none keener than Margaret, who was always the first to turn up with her secondhand racquet in one hand, her two shillings in the other, and loads of determination.

Margaret had already changed her game from hitting with her natural left hand to her right hand. The boys in her gang had teased her incessantly that there were never any good 'southpaw' players. Needless to say, her backhand was always far more formidable than her forehand, for in playing it she was on her natural side.

Tennis began to consume her: she lived only for the time when she could get out there and hit a ball on the court or against the garage wall, or even one hanging from a rope in a tree.

It was a passion her school teacher didn't share. She confronted Margaret daily with the fact that she needed to get on with her studies and forget this 'tennis madness'. Tensions erupted the day she hauled Margaret up in front of the class and demanded an apology from her for something she had not done. Margaret refused to apologise; she had told the truth and refused to give in. As the teacher seemed intent on severing her ear, Margaret bolted for the door and ran home, determined never to go back. She hated school and now it was threatening her love of tennis—that she couldn't bear! Indeed, she didn't go back, despite her mother's tears and the headmistress's threats.

Three days later she started attending school in Wodonga, four miles away but across the New South Wales border in Victoria. She had made history—going to school in two states without changing houses! Her new headmistress was supportive and greatly encouraging, seeing Margaret's tennis talent as a great gift from God.

By now she had excelled herself in the tennis clinics run by Wal Rutter. He could see the talent in the youngster and he constantly worked with her himself. Most evenings he would hit with her and coach her, installing in her a new self-confidence. He never took any money for these lessons because he knew the family couldn't afford it, so he let Margaret do little jobs around the courts. She painted the court lines, served drinks and even mowed the lawns. She never forgot his invaluable contribution to her life because it was his perseverance, persistence and sheer doggedness that went into her. When she moved up to play in the country district tournaments, he would upbraid her if she won in three sets instead of two. 'You'll never win Wimbledon with that attitude,' he would always say.

He organised many games for Margaret with the men in the club, for she eventually became so strong that no woman in the district could give her a solid match. They all complained that she hit the ball far too hard for a girl, a complaint that many of her future competitors would make in the years ahead.

This practise with the men forced Margaret to develop an extremely powerful and penetrating serve to allow her to advance swiftly into the net. From here she looked to curtail the rally, because sustaining it would not be to her advantage as she was not as physically strong as her male opponents. Thus was birthed her dynamic volley as she consistently punched away winning cross-court defensive returns. By playing the men, she learnt very early to play in an aggressive, attacking manner every time she took the court. This was the new style of tennis she brought into the game.

Frank Sedgman, the Australian Open Champion in 1949 and 1950, prompted Wal Rutter to send Margaret to Victoria to trial her out in the girls' under-19 championships. He wanted to see her in action. He and Keith

Rogers, a professional coach, felt that she showed excellent potential. So it was decided that Margaret should move to the city to further her tennis career.

A job was organised for her by Frank Sedgman, and Margaret took up a position as a junior clerk in his office. He arranged for her to train at his Melbourne gym under the watchful eye of his head physical culturist, Stan Nicholes, and to have coaching with Keith Rogers.

Margaret was only fifteen when she left home to go to Victoria. She took a suitcase, a racquet and a hand-sewn tennis outfit to be worn in her first tournament. Her mother was devastated to think of her daughter going off to play tennis. Her father encouraged her all the way. Their tears at the railway station were hard to contain as they said their goodbyes.

Margaret's move to Melbourne was not as traumatic as it might have been, for she was able to move into the same boarding house as her elder sister, June. June had earlier moved to the city for work, and she provided Margaret with all-important family support. Margaret is aware that without June's encouragement she may never have realised her greatest ambition.

That ambition was to become the first Australian woman to win Wimbledon. Whenever she felt a little discouraged or homesick, she kept that vision before her all the time. She disciplined herself to keep the picture alive in her imagination; it was all she ever really thought about. It was such a burning desire that it consumed every difficulty in the way.

Right from her first appraisal in the gym with Stan

Nicholes, Margaret recognised that to become the best she would have to be the fittest, strongest woman ever to play. One look at her twiggy frame confirmed that this meant a lot of intense, painful work to achieve the strong skeletal structure she would need to play her powerful serve and volley game.

Stan devised a specific tennis movement and physical weight training program involving circuits. Keith Rogers worked with her, doing the same athletic conditioning, which involved long runs to strengthen her aerobic threshhold and short sprints to quicken her reflexes and increase her anaerobic uptake. Margaret became such a good sprinter that she was tempted to concentrate on athletics as a career. Both Stan and Keith were always ready to help Margaret, and again, she never forgot the input of these men into her tennis. There were no monetary rewards: they simply did it to help a talented young Australian achieve her destiny.

Day by day, week by week, she trained so hard that even the men in the gym found it hard to keep up with her. As the slim figure of a girl began to change into the shape of an athlete, Margaret was worried that she would lose her femininity. But assured by Stan that she did not have enough testosterone, the male hormone, to develop bulging muscles, she kept on with the weight program.

Slowly she gained competitive experience, and by her sixteenth year she had managed to take all before her in most competitions, except for one other outstanding junior, Jan Lehane.

Then in 1960, just two-and-a-half years after the shy

teenager began her earnest preparation to contest the Australian title for the first time, she actually won it! Not only did she win it, but she also managed to beat the world champion at that time, Maria Bueno, in three sets. She was delighted, but she could see the face of a beaming Wal Rutter saying, 'You should have beaten her in straight sets if you want to be the first Australian woman to win Wimbledon'.

The seventeen-year-old was famous overnight. But with that victory came the enormous pressure to play up to the same standard and prove it was no fluke, a one-off victory she could never repeat. Immediately afterwards, during the New Zealand tour, she lost the final of the New Zealand Open. For the first time she was playing under the pressure of expectations that she should be winning even if she was not. Previously that had never worried her.

It was immediately decided that in reality she had won the Australian 'before' her time. As Frank Sedgman commented, 'I knew she was good, but not that good'. He had always told her he believed she could be the first Australian woman to win Wimbledon, but not even he had expected her to excel at such a rapid pace.

So, after consultations with the 'powers that be'—the Lawn Tennis Association of Australia (LTAA)—she was not selected to go on the tour with the rest of the Australian team in 1960.

She was devastated by this. It was a blow to her pride and she was severely disappointed not to be going overseas and having a chance to win Wimbledon. She had proved herself: this was grossly unfair.

The LTAA felt she was immature and needed more time. Margaret did use the time well, training and conditioning herself to a state of near physical perfection. Determination saw she would never be left out again.

CHAPTER 2
THE AMAZING AUSSIE AMAZON

Winning the Australian Open for the second successive year in 1961 assured Margaret of a place in the Australian team to tour Europe, England and the United States. The vision of Wimbledon was so much closer and she was still only a teenager. However, nothing could have prepared her for the nightmare tour she would endure under the authority of the Lawn Tennis Association of Australia's team manageress, Mrs Nel Hopman.

Even before she left Australia's shores for the first time, Margaret was a little apprehensive about Mrs Hopman's statement that she would bring the team home showing a profit on the budget sheet. Tennis in Australia, as in the rest of the world, was still an amateur sport, and appearance money for top players was about the only way a team could profit from touring certain countries. Margaret was aware that, of the five women players in the team, she was the only one who held a Grand Slam title. So where was the profit going to come from?

Their first stop in Monte Carlo at a luxurious castle with servants was like a fairytale world to Margaret. She had never lived in such luxury. It did not hinder her game, however, and she went on to win the Monte Carlo Open.

But in France, the second scheduled city of their tour, the Cinderella-to-riches bubble burst. The team was accommodated in third class hotels in Nice, Aix-en-Provence and Paris. A continental breakfast of croissants and coffee was all they were allowed; it was part of the cheap package deal. Margaret, who was used to a huge breakfast of a grill and eggs, toast, juice and cereal, did not relish the meagre menu.

One night in Paris the team finally revolted and ordered steak and eggs for dinner instead of the usual hotel special. A stiff reprimand followed, and the meal expenses were taken from the players' own pockets. Margaret couldn't believe the treatment the players were receiving. She felt Mrs Hopman was going too far by not providing suitable food for active athletes.

In London it grew worse. More cheap accommodation followed, miles from the courts. There was no allowance for the players to attend doctors, physiotherapists or masseurs for muscle soreness. Practice session after practice session was ordered. This was no pleasure trip they had come away on: it was all hard work and there was no leisure time.

Margaret was tired and grew ill. She became dreadfully homesick. She had no one on the tour to relate to; her best friend and doubles partner, Mary Rectano, had badly injured her foot and been sent back to Australia.

It was considered too expensive to keep her with the team. No wonder this tour was going to return a profit!

Margaret's first Wimbledon was fast approaching, but so were the tired and listless symptoms that she had first noticed in Paris. Her nervous debut was made as the very first match on centre court. She managed to win that day and played well enough to go right through to the quarterfinals. But the English press was out in force to find the Achilles heel of the one they dubbed the 'Aussie Amazon', and her extreme attack of nerves had not escaped their notice.

Margaret took to her bed. She was depressed and despondent. The tour had been such a horrid experience and now she was actually physically ill. She competed in the doubles with her long-time junior rival, Jan Lehane, only to lose to the Americans. Again she took to her bed. This time a doctor was called and she was diagnosed as suffering from glandular fever.

She spent the night of the Wimbledon Ball—the night she had dreamed about—in the University College hospital. She cried to think of her beautiful black and white dress, specially purchased for the occasion, still packed in her suitcase. She also cried because she felt so alone. Her family and friends were thousands of miles away. She had dropped six kilos in weight and was a shadow of her former self.

A lonely nineteenth birthday was spent in the hospital despite the staff making her a birthday cake and Neale Fraser and Rod Laver stopping by to cheer her up. She had lots of time during this period to think, and she decided that she would never again tour with the

Australian team while Mrs Hopman was the manageress.

She only played one more doubles tournament, and that was in Germany, under pressure to make the budget more profitable by money guaranteed for her appearance. She loved the United States and enjoyed the crowds because they were so friendly and enthusiastic. It was also the last part of the tour; this was the homeward run and she knew her days of being treated badly as a player were about to end. She reached the semifinals of the US Open—a magnificent effort after all she had been through, and one which made her one of the world's top four players.

Great controversy surrounded Margaret when she returned to Australia. The press had already caught hold of the friction and strike action of the Australian team on tour, and Margaret's declaration never to go away again under these conditions was fuel for their pens.

The headlines boomed: TEENAGE TENNIS STAR DEFIES TENNIS BRASS. The commotion died down, but the full impact came months later when Margaret faced a full LTAA inquiry on her own, the other players refusing to lend their support. However, she was determined to hold her ground and refused to compromise her position.

As expected, after her third consecutive win in the Australian title she was named to tour in 1962. She accepted, believing Mrs Hopman would not be named as team manageress. However, a month later she was appointed. Margaret felt cheated and deceived by the false assurances given to her. Now, for the sake of her principles, she had to make a decision which could affect her personal tennis career. If she refused to tour, her amateur status may be affected because she would then be considered a professional. It was her against the establishment as she decided to go it alone.

A Melbourne businessman, Robert Mitchell, came to her aid, offering to finance this 'rebel with a cause' on a private tour. However, the LTAA was not about to let their number one player slip away without public censure. It expressed confidence in Mrs Hopman and deplored the embarrassment the controversy had caused her. One official publicly stated that he wished Margaret all the ill-luck in the world and hoped she would lose every tournament she played in.

Despite all the furore, Margaret coped quite well. She had a maturity well beyond her years, perhaps the result of leaving home at fifteen. She was confident she had done the right thing. She and Mrs Bill Edwards, the wife of the president of the Queensland Tennis Association, left for their own private tour one day before the official team left in April 1962.

However, the pettiness of the LTAA went further. On her first attempt to arrange a practice match with one of the Australian girls she was told that there was a ban on anyone practising with her. She was ostracised and cut off from them all. Margaret's determination grew with this rejection, but it still hurt her. She cocooned herself in an isolated world—her racquet alone would show them.

And show them it did. With a valiant Alf Chave, the

Australian men's manager, by her side to help and support her, she won the Italian Open against her old rival, Maria Bueno from Brazil. She was the first Australian to do so. Mr Chave received a 'please explain' letter as to why he had supported her in light of the team ban. His simple but poignant reply—'Because we are both Australians'—received no answer. Not surprisingly, he was never appointed manager again.

From here she went on to take the French Open from Lesley Turner, the official team's number one player. The road to Wimbledon was wide open. She had won ten tournaments in a row. Could she now win this much-coveted crown?

She went into the event as the number one seed, having already won the Australian and French titles. The press was merciless in its approach to her. CAN SMITH WIN WIMBLEDON? one headline questioned. SMITH'S CENTRE COURT NERVES screamed another, remembering her last nervous showing at Wimbledon. Every headline she read reinforced her own fear of failure.

In 1962 the Wimbledon draw only seeded eight players. Margaret's worst fears came to pass when she saw her draw for the first time. She had to play the number three ranked American, Billie Jean Moffit (later Mrs King), in the very first round. Again the press pounced. They played on the bombastic openness of the American, and she was more than happy to admit that Margaret had all the pressure and that she had nothing to lose and everything to gain. And indeed she was right.

Further doubts crept into Margaret's heart as the

press hounded her with constant questions about whether she was nervous playing Billie Jean. She was, but of course she couldn't say so; their hint that an upset was brewing had already marked her mind. It got so bad that Margaret felt physically ill. The nerves were back and she knew she would not play well. True to her fears, she created history by being the first number one seed at Wimbledon to be ousted in the first round. This was the darkest and deepest despondency she had ever felt; it was even worse than the previous year's horror tour.

The next morning, after she had spent a sleepless night reliving every stroke she had played, the newspaper headlines boomed her failure to the world: SMITH LOSES. WILL SMITH EVER WIN WIMBLEDON? She knew how disappointed her family and friends would be at home, and that only made her feel worse.

She felt she had failed herself, her coach and even her country.

Her mother consoled her daughter as best she could over the phone. Although she was upset that Margaret had lost, she was hoping that now she would forget all this tennis nonsense and come home. For the first time Margaret felt her mother may be right. For two years, despite some tremendous wins and many high points, the hurts, frustrations, rejections and disappointments had been almost too much to bear.

But this was only a temporary phase. Telegrams, good wishes and flowers flooded her hotel room, expressing disappointment at her loss but encouraging her that there would be another day. These people believed she still had what it took to be a champion. Champions always get up from a blow; they don't stay down. Particularly precious to her was the following letter she received from England's finest men's player, Fred Perry:

Dear Margaret,
The world seems a lonely place today. With hopes dashed so suddenly yesterday and the circumstances under which you were knocked out of the singles being so dramatic, I am sure you are a most unhappy person. Don't think for one moment you are as alone as you think, for there are many hundreds of thousands of people whose thoughts are with you now.

You have gained the respect and admiration of the world by your attitude in victory and you have also kept that respect by the manner in which you accepted that bolt out of the blue yesterday.

It is one thing to be able to accept success. It is far harder to take defeat, especially when it comes the way it did. Your friends still feel the same way they always felt. The others don't matter—they never did, really. You have probably gained more friends and admirers by the way you accepted this defeat. The quiet way you carried yourself off the Centre Court, even though your heart must have been breaking, will have gained you untold wealth in new friends and admirers.

I say to you don't let it get you down, as I'm sure you won't. There is always another day and at the

age of nineteen, with a tennis game such as yours to back you up, the good days will far outnumber the bad.
Yours sincerely
Fred Perry

Even though she would go on to take the title three times, Wimbledon remained her bogey tournament throughout her career. Had she recognised the negativity of the press lead-up in those first years she would never have paid any heed to it. But now she resolved to reset her sights and put the loss behind her, learning its painful lessons.

Her twentieth birthday was spent aboard the majestic QE2 ocean liner, cruising across the Atlantic to the USA: the country in which she felt very much at home. Most of her finest tennis was played there, for she felt that American crowds appreciated the effort, diligence and determination it took to become the world's top player.

Back home in Australia the crowds never seemed to support her because she was generally the number one seed and rarely the underdog. Australian crowds always liked to support the underdog, regardless of what country they came from. Perhaps it was a throwback to the country's negative self-image as a nation born from the 'rejects and rabble' of nineteenth century British society. It was a 'them and us' mentality, and as she had become a tall poppy in Australian society, she was always vulnerable to having her stem cut out from under her.

Americans applauded and enthusiastically voiced

their approval; they became part of the match. Australian crowds were there merely to spectate, to see a show, just like a Melbourne Cup outing with the players replacing the horses. Likewise in England: the players' skills and talents were often secondary to the attendance of royalty, the latest fashions and the chance to be seen consuming vast quantities of 'strawberries and cream'.

So arriving in America she felt renewed, confident and totally at peace. She had a new goal: to prove she deserved the number one world ranking despite her Wimbledon defeat. In front of 15,000 people at Forest Hills she played Maria Bueno in the semi-final. She knew the crowd was not behind her that day for the Americans loved the graceful Brazilian; but despite the parochial support, Margaret was able to win her way into her first ever US Open final. There she met Darlene Hard, the title holder. Darlene had been beaten by Margaret earlier that year in Sydney and had vowed to avenge her defeat when she got Margaret on her home turf. Now she had her chance. But Margaret's grim determination to be the first Australian woman to win the US Open was something Darlene hadn't counted on. Moreover, if she won, it would partially compensate her for losing Wimbledon and prove she could compete in the big matches. And a big match it was! But Margaret outplayed and outlasted the aggressive Hard to take the match in three sets. She was delighted—but once again she could see Wal Rutter shaking his head and saying, 'You have to win in straight sets if you want to win Wimbledon'.

She returned home to Australia in 1962 to a hero's

welcome. She was dutifully awarded a civic reception: the whole of Albury turned out to welcome their famous daughter home. She had won three of the four Grand Slam tournaments; only Wimbledon had escaped her. It was a superb climax to a year in which she became the first Australian woman to win at Rome, Paris and Forest Hills. She often wondered how the official who wished her ill-luck felt; it was obvious his prayers were not being answered.

Wimbledon did not elude her for long. In fact, the very next year an elated Margaret Smith won the coveted title for the first time, beating Billie Jean Moffitt 6–3, 6–4. Now she could see a smiling Wal Rutter: 'See, I told you you'd only win if you won in straight sets!'

The next year, 1964, she lost her title to Maria Bueno, then regained it from her in 1965. The only title to elude Margaret and stop her from completing a Grand Slam in 1965 was the French Open, in which she was runner-up.

In 1966 she tried to take a third Wimbledon Crown after winning her seventh Australian title in succession. She was unsuccessful, going out in the semi-finals. She then made a startling decision to retire; in hindsight a little premature, for she was only twenty-four years of age and her best tennis was still ahead of her in terms of experience, strength and temperament.

But she had had enough. Her heart was not in it anymore, and she felt it was time to do something other than play tennis for a time. She had lost her vision and had no new goals. She was perishing in a sea of doubt as to why she was playing. Her mother would be delighted.

Margaret always believed she would retire from the sport when she began to lose more than she won. That started to happen in 1966 and culminated in her shock Wimbledon semi-final loss to Billie Jean. She was bored with tennis; it had become robotic and stale. The constant grind of travel, different hotels, never-ending practice sessions and the pressure of championship matches had taken its toll. Tennis no longer stimulated her sense of challenge. She had captured every crown she had gone after.

Perth was the city to which she retired. It was isolated and had a tremendous climate. She could live there in relative obscurity, out of the glare of the publicity that always surrounded her. Even at twenty-four she had never shaken off her shy, gawky, country girl image— at least in her own mind. Interviews and public speaking were the last thing she ever wanted to do. The quality in her that was often labelled arrogance was in reality nothing more than an acute case of shyness.

In Perth she moved in with a well-known sporting family, the Plaisteds, having become a close friend of their daughter Helen as a teenager in Melbourne. Helen was also on the tennis circuit, being one of Western Australia's leading players. Helen and Margaret had often spoken about setting themselves up in the sporting clothes business once their tennis days were behind them. Now the two young hopefuls established a business in the ritzy Perth suburb of Claremont and called it 'The Peep Hole'. Another friend, Anne

Edgar, a physical education teacher, joined them and they all eventually moved into a large Claremont house which Margaret had purchased for $10,000. For the first time in her life, Margaret had lots of dates and went to parties, drank beer and danced many a night away. Tennis seldom crossed her mind and no one reminded her of it. That was just the way she liked it.

She first met Barry Court, her future husband, as part of a group of friends who were constantly together. Barry invited her to his yacht club dance. She didn't really want to go, but was finally coerced into it by Barry's insistence.

She soon learnt that Barry didn't take no for an answer at any time. He was fun-loving and adventurous and loved the water, as she did. His six-foot two-inch frame stood head and shoulders above her, one of the rare individuals who did. They made an outstanding couple.

Barry had all the happy-go-lucky ways of a true extrovert, and he brought Margaret out of her shyness. His gregarious father, Sir Charles Court, had an exuberance for life and an ageless vitality, despite his fifty-odd years, that saw him remain as Premier of Western Australia for a record twenty years. His mother, Lady Court, was a down-to-earth woman who took everyone on face value; she was never impressed by who someone was supposed to be. When meeting Margaret for the first time she warmly welcomed her into her home and asked her whether she knew that she had the same name as that famous tennis player. Within six months the couple were married.

With marriage came a new perspective. Margaret wanted Barry to meet the friends she had made all over the world, and to see the places she had seen and experience the life she had led as a touring tennis player. It was decided that they would go away on a type of honeymoon, with Margaret playing the odd tournament or two as they travelled.

Now she was enthused again. She knew that having Barry beside her would solve most of those lonely, lost feelings that she had encountered when travelling by herself on the circuit. She now had someone special who would be 100 per cent behind her. She intended to only go for the year and then go touring, but her sensational comeback changed all those plans.

During her fourteen months away from the game she had put on weight, but she still had a relatively good standard of fitness because she had taken up squash. In fact, she had become the number two West Australian player behind Helen Plaisted (now Helen Muir), the number one. Brian Bowman, a businessman and top tennis player in Perth, helped her by hitting regularly with her. It took hard work and diligence, but Margaret got back into it with a renewed vigour, now that she had someone she loved to show how well she could play tennis.

They decided to go abroad after she made the final of the Australian Open in Melbourne in 1968. Barry was a tremendous help; he became adept at booking hotels and plane reservations and handling luggage— all the things Margaret was glad to abandon. It left her totally free to concentrate on tennis.

By the time she was due to play in England after touring South Africa, tennis had gone Open and amateurism was dead. It was a happy coincidence, for in that year Margaret went on to make more money than she had in all the previous years combined.

Her comeback year proved promising, and with her win in the first truly Open Australian championship in 1969—the first leg of the Grand Slam—she decided to tour again. Right on target she won the French Open for the third time and then set herself for Wimbledon. But once more she was thwarted in her jinxed tournament. An incredibly fit and powerful Anne Jones beat her in the semi-finals and went on to win the title, becoming the first English player, man or woman, to do so since 1961.

Immediately afterwards, Margaret again avenged that devastating loss by taking the US Open, giving her three out of the four Grand Slam events for the third time in her career. She was frustrated at having come so close to the Slam once again and set her sights so that nothing would stop her taking it the following year. She had the fire back in her belly; she knew the Slam was there; she hoped it would only take one more year.

And it did. The year 1970 became the greatest of her tennis career as she achieved the one goal that had eluded her grasp.

First the record books for the Australian Open were rewritten as Margaret captured her ninth Australian title to set herself off on the first leg of the Slam. Next was the French Open. It was so important that Margaret flew to Los Angeles for a week of secret coaching to straighten out some hitting problems she was experiencing. It paid off as her confidence was restored and she cruised to take her fourth French title.

Now she had two of the four under her belt, but she remained only cautiously optimistic. She had been in this position three times before. She went into the Wimbledon tournament as the number one seed after winning the Queens tournament—the curtain raiser to Wimbledon—and with her old rival Billie Jean as the number two.

True to their seedings they met in the final. It was a battle of the heavyweights of tennis. Neither player was totally fit—Margaret had a badly injured left ankle and Billie Jean sported a knee bandage. But despite their injuries the two fought the longest women's game in Wimbledon history, lasting two hours and twenty-seven minutes.

It was a match of equals. Both players had the iron will and determination that made them champions. But only one could win and truly be called the number one in the world. The gutsy Billie Jean was determined it would be her, but so was Margaret.

Margaret disliked playing Billie Jean because of her constant verbal retorts—a form of gamesmanship that she had brought into the game but which Margaret found off-putting. However, she always respected Billie Jean's great talent, a respect which was obviously mutual, for when Billie Jean was later asked who she hated to play and why, she replied, 'Chris Evert and Margaret Court—just because they were who they were'.

The sparks flew on centre court that day. It was like

'Gunfight at the OK Corral' as the big guns of tennis fired their best shots at each other. The first set lasted a full hour and a half, with Margaret finally taking it 14–12 (there was no tie-breaker operating then). Another hour passed before she finally threw off the jinx of Wimbledon centre court nerves to take the second set 11-9 and her third Wimbledon title.

The press, once derogatory, now hailed her amazing performance. The tennis public hailed Margaret Court as the 'Queen of Queens'.

With the third leg of the Grand Slam now hers, all that remained was the US Open, her favourite tournament. It was only two months away. Her ankle injury had still not healed going into the championship, and her doctors advised her to withdraw or risk permanent injury. But Margaret was not about to let a sore foot rob her of her long-awaited goal.

She advanced easily through to the final without further mishap, but the mental pressure became horrific. She was within one match of the long-awaited Slam, and no one was about to let her forget it.

Rosie Casals was the other finalist that day, but all interest centred on Margaret. Could she finally take the Grand Slam after her ten-year endeavour? Casals seemed set to cause an upset when, with the American crowd obviously behind her as their compatriot, she played extremely well to equalise the match by winning the second set 6–2 after Margaret had taken the first 6–2.

But Margaret steadied, tightened up her concentration and prayed for help. This was the most crucial set of her life. She remembered the pain of earlier losses at Wimbledon and she was not about to leave this court the same dejected way. She would leave a winner; she didn't care how long she had to play to do it. As it turned out it didn't take long. She powered her way through the third set, winning it 6–1 to take the US Open and her long-anticipated Grand Slam.

Margaret had finally fulfilled her desire to return to the number one position and win the Grand Slam. Her victories encouraged her to keep playing, and she and Barry decided to tour again in 1971. In her usual style, she started the year with a win in the 1971 Australian Open. But her hopes of a second Slam were dashed when she failed to win the French Open. Next was Wimbledon, but with the Grand Slam no longer possible, the motivation had partly gone.

Margaret played well to reach the final, where her opponent was another Australian, Evonne Goolagong. But then she went completely off her game. Her coordination and timing were so bad that she stood at the net and let balls that she would normally volley away for winners go straight over her head to land comfortably in by at least two feet! She had gone 'walkabout', the trait so often attributed to her opponent, who was of Aboriginal descent.

Evonne did not face her idol at her best that day, and she knew Margaret was not her usual powerful self. She cleverly exploited Margaret's unexpected inability to serve and volley and richly deserved her popular win. Margaret, although unhappy at losing in such a bewildering manner, was glad to see the cheerful face of

Evonne receive the coveted Wimbledon trophy after an all-Australian final. Evonne had always been a fair competitor, and everyone loved the simple, unassuming girl from the Australian bush.

For weeks before this match Margaret had complained to Barry that her beer had tasted bitter (she often enjoyed a few cans of Fosters after her matches). Feeling nauseated and off balance, a trip to the doctor confirmed what she had begun to suspect: she was three-and-a-half months pregnant.

It was a happy occasion, even though it came at an inopportune time. But it was also sad, as Margaret's mother had died ten days before she knew her daughter was pregnant. Margaret withdrew from the US Open, and she and Barry went home to Perth to await the birth of their child.

Daniel arrived in March 1972. This was something special and new. But Margaret was not yet ready to swap her tennis racquets for domestic life. She hadn't finished; she knew she had more to give. And now she had a new vision. She wanted to be the first mother to become the world's number one. There was another fire burning in her belly.

CHAPTER 3
NUMBER ONE IN THE WORLD

Margaret's first major result in her relentless comeback trail was a semi-final berth in the 1972 US Open, six months after she had given birth to Daniel. Now she had her sights set on another possible Grand Slam in 1973 which would automatically place her as the undisputed number one and achieve her aim of being the world's first professional tennis mum.

Her win in the 1973 Australian Open, her eleventh title, followed by the capture of the French Crown, put her well on the way to achieving the Grand Slam once again. But as always she was cautious, for her infamous bogey tournament, Wimbledon, was still ahead. And once again it proved to be just as she feared, not her happiest playing ground. Another future champion, a young and talented Chris Evert, put her out in the semi-final. And to prove it was as much a nervous, ingrained stigma as Chris's pure playing brilliance, Margaret bounced straight back to take the US Open to win three out of the four Grand Slam events for 1973.

She had achieved her goal of becoming the world's

first tennis playing mother in less than a full year after her baby's birth. To come back at a time when mothers were thought to be better off at home was a great statement of her strength and resilience. She also proved that there is life after pregnancy!

Motherhood seemed to agree with Margaret as she began to play a more relaxed and confident style of tennis. She was content to take things as they came and found that she did not get upset as easily as she had previously.

In the light of her 1973 achievements, 1974 promised to be the year when she would totally dominate the game. She was playing confident, bold tennis—she had at last learned always to rely on her powerful serve and volley game. This came as a result of the most disappointing match she ever played.

It was a 1973 challenge match televised to millions around the world. The challenger was fifty-five year old Bobby Riggs, a former Wimbledon men's champion. He so belittled women's tennis that Margaret felt she needed to stop him dead in his tracks. She believed women's tennis should not be judged according to men's standards. She was no great feminist defender of women, preferring to keep politics out of tennis. She accepted his challenge more because he irritated her immensely.

Little thought or preparation went into her lead-up to the game as she believed him to be an ageing has-been who couldn't hit the ball hard. But she was not prepared for the shrewd gamesmanship he used against her. True to his showman image, he employed tactics that totally destroyed the confidence she had felt going into the match. Her own pre-match morning was spent fishing the only pair of tennis shoes she had brought with her from the toilet bowl into which they had been carefully placed by Daniel, now a toddler. Getting them dry took the remainder of the morning.

She was unaware that the Sunday of the match was Mother's Day in America until she turned up at the San Diego court. There, with all the flamboyance of a theatrical performance, Riggs presented her, 'the nicest mother in the game', with a lovely bunch of red roses. The red was appropriate because Margaret was seething under this patronising performance. Cameras as numerous as people were dotted all around the court, and this unexpected media attention (all invited by Riggs) also upset her.

Suddenly the game was more than just a personal score to be settled, fought out in an out-of-the-way court. It had attracted international media attention. Now she carried the expectations of millions of women all over the world who hoped she would put this loud chauvinist in his place. She realised they would all be watching. And as usual, once she became nervous her powerful, dominating game suffered. It was universally recognised that she was the strongest and best all-round woman player ever to take the court, but she was not the best 'match' player in highly tense situations. Riggs knew this tension to be her Achilles heel and took full advantage of it. She tightened up to such an extent that she later had trouble remembering anything about the game. Riggs totally swamped her in two straight sets, 6-2, 6-1, and happily pocketed the winner-take-all prize money. Margaret was thankful it had been so quick.

It didn't matter in terms of seedings, but in terms of pride she was devastated. Why didn't she play her own game that day? She just didn't know. But one thing she was sure of: she would never again go out and start potting the ball around as she had against Riggs. Her game now was to go out and hit with all the power and strength she had acquired over the years so that no one would beat her in the same way again. And true to her word, she saw out the rest of the 1973 season in dominating form that cemented her further as the world's top player.

Nineteen seventy-three was also a time of great change for Margaret in her personal life. During the French Open in May she had been to a church service in Paris, and she vividly recalls sitting in the service thinking there had to be more to knowing God than simply being in church.

She had no sense of God being real or personal to her. He was somewhere 'up there'. She felt like a dried up river bed. There was no flow of life within her. She sat in the church and prayed that God would reveal himself to her in some tangible way, so that she could really know He was there for her.

The answer to that prayer came later in the year when she was given a book to read by a friend in the US. It was entitled *How to Be Born Again*. Previously, any religious literature given to her had always ended up in the trash can. But for some reason she kept this little book and found herself reading it again and again. Although she did not fully understand its contents, there was something different about it. On her return to Perth in late 1973, she was amazed to hear that her close friend Anne Edgar had become a 'born again' Christian. The change in Anne was as dramatic as anything Margaret had ever witnessed. Her friend was simply radiant and spiritually buoyant on the inside. So it was not long before Margaret accompanied her to a charismatic-style meeting similar to the one where Anne had been so obviously transformed.

At the end of the meeting Margaret responded to the altar call. A man of God challenged all those there about whether they really knew Jesus in a truly personal way as Lord and Saviour. If they did not, they were encouraged to publicly come forward and declare Him to be the Lord of their life. A struggle of infinite proportions went on inside Margaret that night, for she knew that everyone in the meeting would know who she was if she went forward. She was still the world's number one tennis player at the time, and her pride in that, as well as in being a life-long Catholic, almost stopped her moving. But she felt compelled to go out and give her life to Christ, something she knew she had never done before.

It felt as though someone had switched the light on inside. An incredible peace and joy flooded her whole being. She no longer had any doubts about the tangibility of God. He was as real to her as anything she could perceive with her natural senses. He was suddenly so close that the moment of being 'born again' of the

Spirit of God is forever etched in her memory as the greatest day of her life.

Nothing could compare to this wonderful feeling and nothing could take it away from her.

Margaret continued to play tennis through the rest of 1973, all the time knowing that Jesus was with her. She shared her experience with anyone who asked her and was content to grow steadily in the things of God. But in December 1973 she found out she was pregnant again, and she decided against playing until after the birth of her second child. She and Barry and young Daniel went home to Perth to await the arrival of the baby. They were delighted in her second pregnancy, although she felt they could have timed it a little better. Margaret had a great belief that children came as gifts from God—it was more His timing than theirs. (It's a wonder she didn't have a lot more children with an attitude like that!)

Little Marika, her first daughter, was born after a complicated delivery in July 1974. After some worrying days with Marika in intensive care, Margaret was able to take the new addition to the Court household home.

There she became an ordinary wife and mother, with the same everyday chores and pressing problems as every other housewife. Tennis seemed a long way away, but she was still making decisions inside. Could she make it back again? Was she too old?

She really didn't know what to do, and while she stayed at home being a mum, she enjoyed the company of her two closest friends, Helen and Anne, who now had young children of their own.

Eventually Margaret made the decision to return to tennis, knowing that she still had more to offer. She had been in the prime of her career when Marika was born and she felt strong enough to cope with the demands of tough tournament play despite being the mother of two young children, one only a few months old.

In late 1974 she decided to 'test the waters' by playing in South Africa. Her form was promising, and although she did not win the Open singles—that honour went to Kerry Melville, another Australian—she teamed with her young protegé Di Fromholtz to finish as runner-up in the doubles and went home winner of the mixed doubles. Since she had acquitted herself well considering the shortness of her preparation, she and Barry decided to tour once more in 1975, taking both children and a nanny along with them.

Her return in early 1975 to play the Australian Open was not as easy as her first comeback. She was now thirty-three years of age, and the demands of childbirth had taken their toll on her ligament elasticity and general muscle strength. She called on the wizardry of her old Melbourne trainer, Stan Nicholes, to help prepare her for the rigours of tournament play. Margaret was merciless in her preparation, driven by the new goal of making a successful comeback for the second time. She ran, jogged and lifted weights, and although not extremely confident, she entered the Australian Open despite not having competed in a Grand Slam event for over a year.

She made it to the quarter finals, an amazing feat considering the factors against her, but there her progress was halted by a young teenager, Martina Navratilova from Czechoslovakia. After the game, Margaret predicted that Martina would one day be the top player in the world. She could see in Martina the same raw talent, courage and sheer determination which had always characterised her own game. She sensed a new breed of tennis champion had been birthed in Martina, and in others like Chris Evert and Evonne Goolagong who were making their presence felt in the same way as she, Billie Jean King and Maria Bueno had done. It was inevitable that the youngsters who had idolised and modelled their game on hers would one day beat her, playing just the way she did.

Despite the defeat, Margaret felt she was playing reasonably enough to go overseas once again on the professional circuit. At times she questioned what she was doing and why was she doing it. Perhaps it was the money that she was now earning and could still earn before she retired. Obviously that counted, but the drive seemed to come from something within her that had not been truly solved.

An incredible confusion had started to emerge in her: she couldn't seem to equate her new Christianity with her old aggressive style of play. She believed that to win she had to be aggressive, tough and relentless, but she felt she couldn't reconcile these attributes with more God-like qualities. The 1975 tour seemed to be more fun than before, especially with her family alongside her, but at Wimbledon she finally made a private decision to retire at the end of the year after fulfilling all her scheduled commitments.

Margaret had always recognised that deep within her she had some purpose that was to be fulfilled, and she knew it was no longer tennis. She was about to take a new step into a totally different life that not even she could have anticipated.

God was calling, and she had an incredible thirst to know more about her Christian conversion. The little she did know she had shared willingly throughout the tour with those who had asked her. Sharing Jesus with them excited her in much the same way as tennis had done in her early life.

Her priorities had definitely shifted. She recognised that the transition had come because she could no longer visualise her goals as they were no longer centred around tennis. In many ways it was this ability that had taken her from the realm of mediocrity to the brilliant heights of a champion. The world had seen the last of her best tennis, not because she was incapable of repro-ducing it but because she simply had no desire to do so anymore. Her extraordinary love affair with the game would never be over, but this time there would be no going back. The door was finally closed—and a new one was about to open.

On her return to Perth with her family she began to devote more of her time to finding out about the reality of Jesus within her. There was so much she didn't understand, so many things that were incom-prehensible to her. She didn't understand how a God of love could allow so much sickness, suffering and disease in the world. When she herself suffered a mis-carriage, she believed it must have been God's will that she lose the child. An immense dilemma was beginning to develop.

Her heart was zealous for God, but it had long been blinded by religious traditions which made the religious way of life—the deeds, penances and good works—more important than the simple truth of the written Word of God which glorifies Jesus alone.

CHAPTER 4
ACED BY DESPAIR

Margaret retired officially in the latter part of 1975, but she still competed until all her pledged appearances in events, such as the Women's Virginia Slims Tour, were completed in the first part of 1976. Once she had fulfilled these US commitments, she returned to Australia with Barry and the two children to set up home in Perth. They moved back into their stately old home in Claremont, purchased two years before. Margaret was truly excited at the prospect of doing further renovations to make the old residence a real family home. Of course, it already had a tennis court; they wouldn't have bought it otherwise.

Tennis was not totally forgotten as Margaret kept in masterly touch by coaching on the family court. In many ways she did not want to coach, preferring to hang up her racquet for good since she had retired. But she could not escape the feeling that she had so much to offer and needed to use that gift.

'I never accepted any money for the coaching I did,' she confides. 'I just wanted to help anyone who showed some promise to develop their game, and show them how they should structure their training routines to achieve their aims. I never forgot the wonderful start I had, which would never have been possible without the free coaching sessions I received. This was a way I could repay that debt.'

Her coaching sessions soon moved from their Claremont address as she and Barry decided to purchase a wonderful home in Nedlands, high on the hill overlooking the beautiful Swan River, with panoramic views of the city of Perth. It was an idyllic setting considering Barry's love of yachting and her love of the river. And there was lots of room at the bottom of the block to build an enormous tennis court fully equipped with night lights to cater for the proposed social nights of tennis they would have.

Margaret's life was now very full, especially when she became pregnant once more and gave birth to her third child and second daughter, Teresa, in November 1977. At this time, Barry was very busy in the running of the family property near the picturesque town of New Norcia, two hours' drive north-east of Perth. Sheep and wheat were the mainstays on their large holding of five thousand acres. Farming had always been something Barry wanted to do; he had earned his wool-classing qualification with the pastoral company Elders many years before Margaret met him. Now, although they had a full-time manager, Barry was highly involved in the overall management of the farm.

Margaret and Barry had always thought that when she retired they would actually go farming. They both loved the outdoor life. Whenever Margaret was at home on

holidays, taking a break from her hectic tennis commitments, the farm had always provided a perfect retreat.

Barry's absences left Margaret quite a lot on her
own, supervising the three children single-handed. But
as busy as she was being a wife, mother and coach,
Margaret still found time to attend various meetings for
the growth of her Christian faith. She had a compulsive,
driving desire in her heart to know more about the
spiritual aspect of her life. Along with a group of
friends, she attended as many meetings as was humanly
possible. She could not stop thinking about the call she
knew had been on her from the day she asked Jesus
into her life.

'I just wanted everyone to know about Jesus; it was
that simple,' she recalls. 'I needed to know a lot more
myself. There were many questions that I knew I could
not answer. But I did know one thing for certain, that
Jesus was alive and so very real to me. If I died at that
moment I knew I would go to be with Him.' Although
heavily involved in farming, Barry also willingly
assumed the role of babysitter as Margaret pursued her
search, wanting so much to grow in the things of God.

Unfortunately for her, the meetings she attended
often centred around a practice known as 'inner
healing'. She was taught that she needed to go back into
her past life and uncover any suppressed memories of
people and experiences that may have adversely
affected her. She was further told that if these things
weren't worked through and eradicated from her
memory, she would never be truly free and spiritually
mature.

Had she known the scripture in 2 Corinthians 5:17:

*If anyone is in Christ, he is a new creation: old things
are passed away; behold, all things have become new.*

her life would have taken a different direction. But
Margaret did not have any knowledge of the Scriptures,
not having been brought up with them. If she had, she
would have avoided a lot of the heartache and pain she
encountered while trying to dig up the skeletons of her
past and attach some deep, meaningful significance to
them.

Although she sensed that looking back was not really
the way to find the answers she needed, she became
trapped in a merry-go-round of self-examination. One
thing she had learned as an athlete was to always put
the games already played behind and concentrate on the
game ahead. True, she had learnt many valuable lessons
from analysing games, but to dwell on the past meant
certain defeat in the future. Yet as the months went by,
she became more and more absorbed with this 'inner
quest', to the detriment of the rest of life.

'I became totally self-centred with all this emphasis
on looking in at myself,' she says. 'I was not really
aware of my family either, almost to the point of
neglect, as I consistently analysed my life to see why I
felt so guilty, unworthy, fearful and totally insignifi-
cant. My self-esteem crumbled under this type of scru-
tiny. I truly did not even feel human any more. I wept
and cried all the time in a state of emotional distress. I
had nothing to anchor my hope on and floated about

in a sea of bewilderment until I was nothing more than a shipwrecked shell.'

There was not a lot of sound biblical teaching in her life at this time. Margaret found herself hearing many ideas from a variety of speakers but nothing from anyone who had a solid knowledge of the Word of God. She never heard the truth she so desperately needed to hear: that God and His Word are one, and that she needed to build her life on the stability of God's unchanging Word to have any real basis for concrete change.

The more she went into inner healing, the more confused she became. There simply was not a great deal of 'past' for her to dig through to find the reason for her enormous feelings of inferiority and worthlessness. She had always lived a good, moral life before God, and wherever she had played around the world she had gone to church on Sunday if possible. She knew that she had never been really loved as a young child—her mother, although caring, had allowed fear to override her ability to love freely, and her father, like most Australian men of the post-war era, had found it difficult to show real affection to his youngest daughter—but none of these experiences were the cause of her own mammoth fear and insecurity (although she admits they contributed).

The problem was not that she had these insecurities; it was how she was to get rid of them. Looking back all the time only kept her centred on the problems until they became like a stronghold over her mind. There seemed to be no future ahead, and living for today was impossible because the past was always uppermost in her thoughts. The more she tried to forget it, the more her mind bombarded her with a confused tangle of emotions.

Even the normal pride she felt in having been the world's best tennis player was now seen to be a bad thing that she needed to deal with. It was labelled an 'evil spirit' that needed to be cast out of her. This only magnified her fear, for now she had things to deal with she had never considered before. She began to think that she needed to be set free from anything that could even remotely be considered an ungodly part of her life. Over time Margaret began to feel she was in the grip of Satan himself.

Confusion, disappointment and self-hatred took a mighty hold on her life. Fear opened the door to physical illness. Her once powerful, muscular frame became emaciated. Her lack of peace, confused thoughts and resulting emotional instability all took a terrible toll.

'I listened to man, I followed man and I trusted man and did not look to the truth of the Scriptures myself,' she explains. 'I thought that God was a God of judgment and so I prayed for God to break my heart. I felt that He was out to get me, and so I was hitting myself over the head all the time, and I didn't even know it.'

A torn heart valve came as the answer to her 'prayer' to be broken. She felt totally perplexed. What had she done to deserve such a painful answer? Immediately she was put onto heart tablets, with a specialist's diagnosis that she would be on medication for the rest of her life. She felt hurt, lonely and depressed, and could not see any way out of the dark pit she was in.

There were very few people to whom she could turn for help. Not even Barry, who was always loving and supportive, really understood the full depths of the despair she felt. Thankfully she had Anne and Helen, her two closest friends, who did understand and became pillars of strength for her. They would often spend the night with Margaret when Barry was away at the farm. She was terrified of being alone in the dark, for she felt a presence of evil around her that was so real she could almost 'see' grotesque faces laughing at her. Her two friends would sit and pray with her, sometimes all through the night, reassuring her that everything would be fine.

At one stage a 'deliverance' team was assigned to her, but they put so much emphasis on there being a demonic spirit behind every single ailment or feeling that it made her more fearful than ever. She was 'delivered' from spirits of nausea, fear, cramp, insomnia, pride . . . the list was endless. Every time she went to seek help she was relieved of another demon or two. Bewilderment and turmoil ruled her life because she suspected that she had no demons to get rid of in the first place. She was at a dangerous spiritual place—the evil things of the spirit were dreadfully real, but the counterbalancing integrity of the Word of God, which shows the defeat of the forces of darkness and renders them totally harmless to knowledgeable believers, was absent. This type of 'deliverance ministry' was something she finally decided to have nothing more to do with.

Barry did not understand the spiritual torment she was going through and really wanted nothing to do with anything so radical. All he could see was that it had reduced his once outgoing wife to a complete emotional mess, too afraid to live and enjoy life as she had always done before.

There was such torment in Margaret's life that to this day she remembers its awesome power. At times she felt it was like a type of paralysis, leaving her unable to perform the simple, mundane functions of her own household. Her mind was like a windmill turning over and over, with dreadful thoughts flooding her head incessantly. Sleep was only possible with the help of sleeping tablets; her mind just could not stop ticking over. Insomnia became a way of life, and soon severe depression descended over her like a large, black storm cloud.

'When morning came I wished it was night and when night came I wished it was morning,' she relates. 'I had no peace, either awake or fitfully asleep; it didn't matter. I really thought that if it was going to be like this on earth then I would rather go home and be with God. I was of no use to anybody; not to myself, my family or even to God.'

Hearing all the arguments, however logical and rational, as to why such terror was unwarranted did not ease her situation at all. Being told that she had so much to live for, with a devoted husband and family and enough wealth accumulated for the remainder of her life, only produced further guilt, because she knew there was no reason for her to feel the way she felt—but she did!

To Margaret it seemed she was in another world. She

could not see her way out of the mess she was in. To go to the pastors whose teaching she had believed became unthinkable; she knew she would only be subjected to further 'spirits' being cast out of her. She had nowhere to turn.

In 1979 she was hospitalised and treated for a variety of symptoms. This enforced stay gave her time to think and question the direction of her life. It had not gotten any better, but far worse. She knew it should not be this way.

Somehow she sensed that she had been involved in things that were not quite right, and now she decided to put everything on hold. She wanted nothing more to do with any of it.

CHAPTER 5
ESCAPE FROM THE DARKNESS

T he turning point came in Margaret's life not long after she left hospital. Two businessmen told her about a powerful, faith-teaching video they had seen, featuring a prominent pastor from America, Dr Fred Price.

Margaret recognised the name. She remembered that as a new Christian she had been invited to give her testimony at a Full Gospel Businessmen's Fellowship International meeting in Hawaii. She had refused, a little fearful of public speaking, until she found out that Dr Price was going to be the guest speaker. She had heard some wonderful things about his ministry back home in Australia and really wanted to hear him speak.

In that meeting, Dr Price, acting on a word of knowledge, prophesied that God was healing someone in the audience of stomach ulcers at the very time he was speaking. That someone was Barry, who told Margaret about it some hours later. To Margaret this was very good news, because it meant she would no longer have to be careful about the type of food she served Barry; he could eat anything. The only thing that disappointed her was that she thought Barry would be so excited by the healing that he would give his life to Christ immediately, but he did not. Thus she experienced a scriptural truth that Jesus often taught: that seeing or even experiencing a miracle will not necessarily make someone a believer. Believing is always by faith, and obviously Barry had not yet reached that faith level.

Now, some years later, the name Dr Fred Price had come to her attention again. What really excited her was the fact that she had been told about his video by two men who had no idea she had already seen and heard this man and been very impressed by his faith message, even back then.

As she sat and watched the video—the first thing she had even attempted to touch with a 'Christian' message for months—she felt as though she was hearing something positive and uplifting for the very first time. She knew that she had been exposed to this dynamic teaching back in Hawaii all those years before, but she obviously had not been ready to absorb it. She felt as though a light switch had been turned on inside her. She heard clearly for the first time that the Word of God was the only way to grow in faith and to overcome the areas of defeat in life. She sat transfixed, took pages of notes and studied the scriptures he gave.

In 1979, Margaret began to attend a newly formed church in Perth which taught along the same lines as Dr Price. The Word, as found in the Bible, was its sole reference and foundation. 'If you can't find what I teach you in the Word, then disregard my message,' the pastor would tell his congregation. It was here that

Margaret learnt that she needed to find scriptures relevant to her needs and put them into her life to bring about change. She sensed that her answers were all tied up with really understanding which scriptural words she needed.

The words she found were as vital to her as was the discovery by Martin Luther of his life-changing scripture, 'The just shall live by faith' (Romans 1:17). Not only did this scripture turn his whole life around but it affected a whole church age. The scripture Margaret found was in 2 Timothy 1:7:

> For God has not given us a spirit of fear, but of power and of love and of a sound mind.

The discovery of this scripture at that time turned her whole life around forever.

At first this was the only scripture she could memorise entirely because her mind was still very confused. Over and over she said it; day and night, night and day. She personalised it: 'God has not given me the spirit of fear, but of power, and of love, and of a sound mind.' She constantly repeated it when fear, doubt and confusion tried to take back the small amount of ground they had lost to this positive affirmation. It was beginning to push them from their stronghold over her mind. The more she spoke it, the more her mind began to believe what she said—and slowly it began to act as if it was so.

Somehow—she did not really know how—the fear started to diminish. Her mind stopped spinning in circles. Now she was able to read and memorise further scriptures. She began to take the Bible as her 'spiritual medicine', just as she was still taking her physical medication. She learnt that as she was speaking scriptural statements over herself daily, she was washing herself in the water of God's Word. Slowly she sensed many other areas of her life also changing, and it was all good.

Margaret listened to lots of other people's testimonies and heard the good news that Jesus had healed and restored them, making them complete people. She felt that if God had done all that for others, He would do it for her. She found a scriptural truth behind this reasoning:

God is no respecter of persons. (Acts 10:34, KJV)

What God did for one person He must do for anyone who operates the necessary principles. Margaret had a zealous desire to find out just how these godly principles worked. The testimonies she heard encouraged her, and for the first time she sensed there was a way out of the mess she was in.

Although she was still physically ill, tired and drained, with too many worries and cares, she knew that the fearful torment was no longer there. Over and over again she kept repeating, 'God has not given me the spirit of fear, but of power, and of love and of a sound mind'. In this she learnt she was acting on another scriptural principle, that

Faith comes by hearing, and hearing by the Word of God. (Romans 10:17)

This was the start of her growth in faith, speaking of things that were not, as though they were—and not looking at the natural evidence which said she did not have 'power, love and a sound mind'.

Since Margaret did nothing else for the next few months, it was inevitable that her faith level would develop. She had at last stumbled on the scriptural formula for the growth in faith she had always earnestly desired:

> Now faith is the substance of things hoped for, the evidence of things not seen. (Hebrews 11:1)

She began to stabilise her thought life and bring it under the transforming effect of the Word. The Bible contained a wealth of wisdom on how she could keep her mind centred on God and remain in perfect peace. She had once thought this impossible, but no longer.

Her diligence during her tennis years to train and apply herself to the arduous task of getting her body into peak physical condition now paid off. She applied the same diligence to keeping the Word of God before her eyes and in her mouth at all times—especially the scriptures that were relevant to her particular problems. Now she felt she understood clearly why she had suffered so much: she had never read, meditated on and attended to the Word. She was determined that it would never escape her attention again. It held the key to her salvation, healing, wholeness, soundness and general well-being. It was the solid basis on which she had to build her faith.

The Word was to be the 'inner healing' in her life. As she put God's Word into her areas of hurt and concern, it drove out all the grief, unforgiveness and broken-heartedness. Unlike the 'inner healing' practice she tried at first, which simply became a pacifier, the Word actually dealt with the problem. For the Word is health and healing, and it sets you free!

Philippians 4:13 was the scripture that Margaret knew she was to base her faith on for the healing she needed in her body. Daily she repeated it over and over to herself:

I can do all things through Christ who strengthens me.

The more she said it, the more she started to believe it and the stronger she became. The more she repeated it, the more her faith began to rise. She began to add other scriptures relating to healing to her daily confession:

But those who wait on the Lord shall renew their strength; they shall mount up with wings like eagles; they shall run and not be weary, they shall walk and not faint. (Isaiah 40:31)

The scriptures themselves seemed to have a wonderful healing and soothing effect even as she spoke them.

The day the reality came home to her that her faith really had grown through hearing the Word of God is forever etched in Margaret's memory. Her friend Helen had dropped by to pay Margaret a routine visit, as she had regularly done since she had taken ill. She quite innocently remarked that Margaret looked particularly tired that day.

'No, I can do all things through Christ who strengthens me,' Margaret replied, surprising both Helen and herself with this unusually bold statement. The moment the words left her lips she realised that mere hope had gone and had been replaced by a confident sense of 'knowing' that she was healthy, even though she still looked and appeared to be very sick. It was at that time, she realised, that the Word had 'become flesh' in her. 'I knew from that day forward that I would be totally and perfectly healed; it was only a matter of time.'

That healing was not instant, but she began to act as if it had been. She started to step out and go for light jogs and have a hit of tennis. She began to set her home in order and felt capable of doing more things around the house. At times she felt like throwing away her medications, but because there was still a remnant of uncertainty there—and she knew it—she kept taking the drugs prescribed for her heart. Her dependence on sleeping tablets and anti-depressants had almost gone.

The change in her appearance and general demeanour was remarkable, especially to those who had watched her slide into the pit of depression. But she still had a long way to go, and she jumped at the suggestion that she should go to the newly-established Rhema Bible Training Centre to study the Word in a more official and formalised manner.

Margaret wanted to go desperately, knowing that anyone who desired to study God's Word was always in His perfect will. Ultimately, it was a decision that depended on Barry's consent, and with a little bit of powerful lobbying she found herself in the class of 1982. The school had a creche for her two youngest children, Teresa and Margaret's third daughter, Lisa. Danny and Marika were now at school, but the Bible School ran according to the same schedule as the children's school, so Margaret had the same school holidays. Classes were held only from 9.00 a.m. to 12.30 p.m., catering for parents and part-time workers alike.

Bible School was a whole new experience for Margaret. Never before had she been so excited about 'study'. The truths she began to learn astounded her. 'It was as though I had been so blind all those years,' she relates. 'Scales of doubt, unbelief and fear fell off me as I studied the Word of God in an orderly fashion.'

It was in Bible School that she began to understand the incredible power of her own words, for good or ill. Faith-filled words were always positive; fear-filled words were always negative. Without realising it, she had lived for many years under the snare of the words of her own mouth. Very few positive, uplifting words had ever left her lips; she had mostly spoken the same negative words she heard everyone around her use. The world was saturated with negativity; 'good news' rarely made the headlines.

Another thing she started to notice was that any time she did read a newspaper or listen to a news report, invariably the highlight was someone collapsing and dying of a heart attack. In the past, fear had always gripped her and told her that she would be next. Now she refused to listen to bad news, realising that what she heard and saw influenced the way she reacted in her own life. She only wanted to hear positive and uplifting words.

The Word of God, the most positive of all words, had never been put in front of her like this. She was excited to find wisdom in the Bible that explained clearly her own past defeats:

Death and life are in the power of the tongue, and those who love it will eat its fruit. (Proverbs 18:21)

Up until now her words had created 'death', not life. She had constantly spoken about her fears, worries, cares, concerns, illness, guilt, insecurities ... all very real, but all very negative. She immediately began to turn her words around to the positive, speaking the answers she desired by faith. Any time the negative thoughts came, she did not give them any power by speaking them into existence; instead, she thought the exact opposite. God's Word is always the opposite of defeat, despair and discouragement.

Bible School provided her with a wonderful opportunity to feast on the Word of God for three solid hours a day. This 'Word diet' was a scriptural principle, she saw. Just as her natural physical body needed food three times a day, so too her 'spirit man' needed the food of God's Word at least three times daily:

Man shall not live by bread alone, but by every word that proceeds from the mouth of God. (Matthew 4:4)

Many years before, God had told the prophet Hosea: *'My people are destroyed for lack of knowledge'* (Hosea 4:6). And indeed, it had been this same lack of knowledge that had characterised her own life and brought about her defeat. As she studied and learnt the truth of the Scriptures, she felt her mind was being freed daily from the shackles of confusion that had formerly bound it.

Healing took on a whole new significance as she learned that Jesus had died not only to save her, but to heal her body also. The two separate atonements were provided in His one act on Calvary:

But He was wounded for our transgressions, He was bruised for our iniquities; the chastisement for our peace was upon Him, and by His stripes we are healed. (Isaiah 53:5)

To learn that Jesus had taken thirty-nine lashes on His back for all her sicknesses was a great catalyst for her in building up her faith to receive her own supernatural healing.

Eight months passed before she underwent a series of tests, initiated by a doctor friend who lived next door, to check out her heart thoroughly. 'You're in perfect health,' the report came back; 'the torn valve is totally healed.' Today, over seventeen years later, there is still no sign of any heart condition. Margaret is living proof that every promise given in the Word of God can come to pass in the life of anyone who will do as she did—believe the promise of God over the reality of the circumstance.

Margaret began to see that her old preconceptions of God as a stern, harsh judge just waiting to catch her out the minute she missed the mark had distorted her expectations of Him. She had always prayed for His help on match days knowing He was out there some-where, but she had never really been sure that He would answer. He had a large universe to run, and Wimbledon or Forest Hills may not warrant any particular attention that day. If she won, well, that was God's will, and if she lost, well, that was God's will too. He was inconsistent in answering some of her hasty requests thrown up in the midst of the battle and not answering others. Some of the titles she prayed hardest to win were the very ones she inexplicably lost. Not-withstanding the fact that this denied her a considerable amount of satisfaction and delight, she reasoned that God knew what was best for her, even though losing was not high on her list of what she thought was for her 'best'.

That image of God carried over into her life generally. As a diligent church-goer all her life, she had been indoctrinated with the unscriptural yet widely preached doctrine that whatever happened in her life, good or bad, was God's will. If she was healthy, well, God be praised; if she was sick, then God be praised too, because He obviously wanted her sick! Now she realised once and for all that God wanted His children well.

A time of great strengthening and growth occurred in Margaret following the supernatural healing of her heart. She had moved into a higher realm of faith than she had ever known before. She had received earlier healings of a spinal curvature and scoliosis through the scriptural 'laying on of hands' by other believers; but this time her own faith in the written Word of God had brought her the healing she desperately needed. Her faith in the Word on salvation was finally rewarded when Barry gave his life to Christ towards the end of her second year at Bible School. To have all her family present and saved at the graduation ceremony was the best graduation present she could ever have received. The Word had not returned empty when it had been spoken over Barry. God's Word never returns to Him without it accomplishing that for which it is sent (Isaiah 55:11).

Margaret graduated in 1983 knowing that ahead was a work to which God had called her, but the time was not yet right. The family took priority over any public ministry, for she knew that her 'ministry' for the time being was her husband and children. Her preparation was never neglected, however, as she spent the next seven years in various 'ministries of helps'—from assisting in the church nursery to counselling, from leading prayer and intercession groups to hospital and home visitation of the sick. Margaret learnt very early that there can be no victory in any facet of ministry without preceding prayer.

'Prayer is direct communication with God; prayer breaks the powers of darkness; prayer is speaking the

Word, the answer, into every situation. Prayer changes things,' she enthuses.

Over the years Margaret began to observe that anyone who genuinely knew how to apply faith and the Word of God to their problems always overcame them. Alternatively, those who did not were often miserably defeated. Therefore it was obvious to her (for she too had learnt the same lesson by experience) that it was only the correct application of faith that assures 'the victory that overcomes the world' (1 John 5:4).

The next chapter outlines the principles that Margaret and others have used to develop their faith into 'winning faith'. These principles do not work for Margaret because she is a famous tennis player or because God has seen fit to give her more faith than anyone else. They work because they are all from the Word of God. They work for Margaret, and in the same way they will work for anyone who understands and correctly applies them.

Margaret has no desire to see anyone suffer the way she did for seven years before learning these principles. No one need walk in a wilderness of defeat, as she did for the first part of her Christian life. 'All it takes is one small step of faith in Jesus to begin the most successful and exciting period of life you can ever experience,' she evangelises. God's own Word says it best:

I call heaven and earth as witnesses today against you, that I have set before you life and death, blessing and cursing; therefore choose life, that both you and your descendants may live. (Deuteronomy 30:19)

Chapter 6
Faith and Victory

The development of faith begins with a simple life-changing decision. The Bible clearly lays out that everyone is faced with a choice between life and death, victory and defeat. There is no middle ground. A person can either choose God and therefore life, or be left with the only alternative, death. The choice is made by accepting Jesus Christ, as Margaret did many years ago, or rejecting Him.

Although Margaret made that all-important decision, she did not know that this acceptance automatically gave her everything she would ever need for a winning faith to develop. She did not fully understand that the seed of faith had been planted in her own re-created spirit and that growth would come by watering that seed with the Word of God.

Margaret's story dispels the theory that only those who are down and out, with no inner strength of their own, seek Christ as a crutch. She accepted Christ when she was number one in the world in tennis—hardly down and out. But it was the lack of knowledge of her righteousness in Christ that saw her life degenerate into defeat. To ensure that the people to whom she ministers do not suffer the same defeat, she consistently teaches this principle of righteousness as being the foundation to faith.

'Righteousness can be easily understood,' she teaches, giving one of her many practical illustrations. 'My children are my children because they have been born from my body. Nothing can ever destroy that relationship I have with them. They have all the rights and privileges of the Court family. This builds into them a healthy self-esteem and feelings of worth; they know they are valuable and precious to us, and everything we have is theirs also. They know that Barry and I would never do anything to hurt them or reject them in any way, regardless of what they may do in their lives. God is the same with every single person who is "born" into His family by accepting the death of His Son, Jesus Christ. Jesus died so that you could live, and He also rose again so that, while you will physically die, you will never spiritually die. He has conquered death, hell and the grave for you. The moment you accept Him in your life, you are immediately adopted into God's family as His very own child. All the rights and privileges of God's family—a wonderful heritage—are now yours. God will never do anything to hurt you and certainly will never reject you once you come to Him.'

Just as a person is righteous (that is, in right standing) in a family because they are born into that family, so when we are born into God's family we are in 'right standing' with Him. This has nothing to do with what we can or can't do in ourselves, but comes because God offers us a place in His family through the 'new birth'.

Understanding that this was her position with God was the key that turned Margaret's life around.

She stresses this principle more than any other she teaches today, because she strongly believes that righteousness is the foundation of faith and no one can have winning faith until they are assured they can go boldly into the throne room of God and find grace and mercy in time of need (Hebrews 4:16). She knows full well, having experienced it herself, that nobody who feels inferior, guilty or worthless will come boldly to God, and that God can only work through faith being activated and released.

Faith comes by hearing, and hearing by the Word of God. (Romans 10:17)

This scriptural principle is vital to the growth of faith. No one had ever told Margaret that her faith could grow and develop by listening to the Word of God. She thought that the trials, tests and experiences of everyday life, whether good or bad, would determine her faith growth. Just as Margaret did not become a successful tennis player overnight, so her faith was not perfected overnight. Now her encouragement to others is always this: 'Read the Word, study the Word and put that Word deep down on the inside of you. Say the Word, hear the Word and keep on hearing the Word.' Her favourite scripture is Proverbs 4:20–23:

My son, given attention to my words; incline your ear to my sayings. Do not let them depart from your eyes; keep them in the midst of your heart. For they are life to those who find them, and health to all their flesh. Keep your heart with all diligence, for out of it spring the issues of life.

True scriptural faith, based on the Word, has to have corresponding action for it to be effective. This was a further principle that helped Margaret receive her own healing—healing that had always been available through God's provision, although she had not known how to appropriate it for her life.

'I learned to speak the answer and never the problem. The answer was always a scripture from the Word of God, so I found all the scriptures on healing and then personalised them. Day by day as I spoke the words into my body, I knew I was not only growing physically much stronger, but my faith for healing was also growing strong. Within months the symptoms began to subside, until finally they left altogether, washed away by the water of God's Word.

'The words of your mouth are so powerful,' she emphasises again and again. 'If you have God's Word in your heart you will speak faith; if not, you will speak fear.'

Looking back to her early tennis career, she readily admits that her life was dominated by fears, cares and worries. 'I often spoke about how I felt and how nervous I was,' she recalls, 'and I always played the way I thought I would. I did not know that even though the negative thoughts had penetrated deep into my heart, I could have aborted them by not speaking them into existence. But instead I birthed them into existence and gave them power through my own mouth. I've since learnt that my thoughts, by themselves, have no power, but once I speak them into the atmosphere I have established either a negative or a positive situation—one in which God is able to be involved or one in which the devil is involved.

'God made you in His image, and He gave you the same ability He has to create things with the words of your mouth,' she explains. 'God created the heavens and the earth by the words of His mouth. Your words instantly reveal your innermost heart beliefs and ultimately will create the world in which you live.'

Margaret firmly believes that too many people speak their problems instead of speaking answers. That is what she used to do until she realised that talking about problems only intensified their hold on her.

'You have to see the answer by faith *before* it becomes a reality,' she explains. 'The tongue is the brush, the heart is the canvas and the Holy Spirit is the oil. The Holy Spirit takes the words we speak and paints a picture on the canvas of our heart. As we keep speaking the Word (which is the answer we desire), that image will be formed in our hearts and eventually we will have what we can "see".

'There is no other way, there are no shortcuts,' she warns. 'God will reward those who diligently seek Him.'

Margaret has never known the meaning of the word 'quit'—it is not a word found in a champion's vocabulary. Winners never quit and quitters never win. She has had many bad experiences in her endeavour to grow in her Christian walk, but she has never given up.

'It is always too soon to quit,' she encourages. 'Even when it looks like nothing is happening, stay with the Word. It will work for you, the same as it does for me. God is no respecter of persons. His Word is for anyone who will get it, read and study it, speak and confess it, eat it and live it and base their whole life on it.

'Faith hears, faith sees, faith speaks, faith acts and faith receives. This is always the way it operates, even in the world system. My success in tennis came by employing these godly principles without even knowing that they were God's principles, established for man to be successful in all that he does.

'Frank Sedgman told me when I was only twelve years old that he felt I could be the first Australian woman to win Wimbledon. I never forgot those words and deep within me they created a belief that one day it might be a possibility. The more I thought about what I had heard, the more I began to see a vision of myself winning at Wimbledon. A blueprint began to form and I could actually see myself out there, playing and receiving the coveted trophy. Years later I found myself saying that I *would* be—not *might* be—the first Australian woman to win Wimbledon. I began to act as if it was so, playing with loads of confidence on the way to my goal, surprising everyone except myself by winning the Australian Open when I was just seventeen.

'The faith I had in my own ability to realise my ultimate goal of winning Wimbledon was greatly enhanced by this unexpected win. However, it would take me another three years to win my first Wimbledon title, despite the fact that I was the top ranked player in the world at that time. The simple truth was that I needed those years to build my faith to really believe, not just hope, that I could do it. I finally achieved that aim in 1963. After this Wimbledon victory, my confidence was high and I knew I could win the highly coveted Grand Slam. And I did that in 1970. It was the greatest thrill of my tennis career.

'The principle here is that what I had faith to achieve was what I ultimately did achieve. Until I really believed I could do it, deep down on the inside of me, I could not do it. In every defeat I suffered, there was always just enough doubt to allow fear to creep in, overtake me and rob me of success.'

Margaret is quick to show that Jesus outlined these same principles many years ago in the gospels. He firstly went about teaching and preaching the good news of the gospel. The people *heard*.

Next He painted a picture for them of how life could be lived and enjoyed here on earth. He gave them a blueprint for their lives and put an expectant hope deep in their hearts. The people *saw*.

Then He made the people speak the faith they had in their hearts back to Him. He wanted them to remind Him of His own words by asking them what they wanted from Him—testing to see if they believed the words He had spoken. And as they affirmed and acknowledged their belief in Him, He was able to move on their faith confession and meet all their expectations. The people *spoke*.

But He always demanded that the faith they had expressed be put into some sort of action. 'Stretch out your hand,' He commanded of the man with the withered arm. 'Rise up and walk,' He instructed the man lame from birth. 'Go and wash the mud from your eyes,' He directed the blind man. 'Go and sin no more,' He gently corrected the woman caught in adultery. The people *acted*.

Then, every time anyone acted on His word, they received their miracle. (It was only recorded that in Nazareth, His own home town, He could do no mighty works because of their unbelief.) The people *received*.

If you can believe, all things are possible to him who believes. (Mark 9:23)

Margaret teaches the same faith principles as Jesus. She has a heart to be more and more like Him every day—to have a ministry that is established on the Word of God and to fulfil the 'great commission' Jesus gave His body of believers:

Go into all the world and preach the gospel to every creature. He who believes and is baptised will be saved; but he who does not believe will be condemned. And these signs will follow those who believe: In My name they will cast out demons; they will speak with new tongues; they will take up serpents; and if they drink anything deadly, it will by no means hurt them; they will lay hands on the sick, and they will recover. (Mark 16:15–18)

Early in 1990, Margaret knew the time had finally come to form her own ministry to fulfil the divine commission Jesus had given to her. It could not be full-time yet as her two eldest children were in tertiary studies and the two youngest were still in secondary school. The Court home still had a full complement of six since none had left home, and Margaret knew they still needed a major part of her time. This she believed was the right order of priority: God first, then family, then ministry. She felt that too many people in ministry had wrongly neglected their families to serve God. Often this neglect had led to broken family units, with the children blaming God for robbing them of a parent who was never there for them, and so rejecting Him. She did not want to make any such mistake.

Even tennis had fallen into the background somewhat since she had decided not to coach anyone two years before, wanting to wisely manage her small amount of spare time as she put her family first. There were simply not enough hours in the day to do everything. Ministry preparation and speaking engagements took up the time she had once spent in coaching tennis.

With Barry and the children fully supportive, her long-awaited move into public ministry had begun.

Chapter 7
A Vision Becomes Reality
Margaret Court Ministries

The establishment of Margaret Court Ministries Inc. in early 1991 was the first official step Margaret took to publicly declare the call of God on her life.

She would have been content to serve God in any capacity that He willed, but she had no doubt that she was to establish a work under her own name. Accordingly, she set up the ministry as a way to achieve the original vision she had been given—to go and proclaim the gospel to all those who needed to hear its good news. All the personal attributes and severe disciplines that had contributed to her phenomenal tennis success were about to be put into her own ministry. She knew she would have to be as determined, single-minded and dedicated to her calling as she had been in her earlier sporting career if she was going to fulfil her destiny.

The ministry she established was an outreach ministry to the city of Perth. Halls, Community Centres and recreational buildings were hired to hold meetings. Margaret wanted to use ordinary community-type buildings which were non-threatening and easily accessible to those without a church background. Her ministry was not a church and was not meant to take the place of a church. Meetings were held mid-week so that the ministry team and the people who came could attend regular Sunday services in their own churches.

In a desire to be accountable, Margaret established a Reference Board of four pastors from different church affiliations around Perth. These men had the same spirit as she did to see the lost won to Christ. She also established an Advisory Board of seven, including two more pastors, to oversee the general running of the ministry. These Boards were set up to ensure that everything was done decently and in order. She welcomed the wealth of wisdom and practical advice that came from them, deliberately making herself answerable to others more mature in ministry than herself.

To further cloak her ministry in a 'covering mantle', she was officially ordained in early 1991 by Pastor Ray McCauley of Rhema Bible Church, South Africa, in the presence of her own pastor, Philip Baker of Rhema Family Church, Perth. She had visited Rhema in South Africa some years before to speak at the church's highly successful sporting night called 'Night of Champions'. She had long respected Ray McCauley—a former Mr Universe finalist in body building—for his uncompromising stand for God, a stand not unlike her own. During South Africa's turmoil in the 1980s he rose to a position of prominence, being one of the few 're-ligious' leaders invited to be present at important peace talks between the various dissenting groups. He proclaimed a call to unity and repentance, believing that South Africa had to seek God as never before as the answer to its ugly racial problems. Just as Ray was called to South Africa, so Margaret felt she was called to her own nation of Australia, to call it to repent and return to God and righteousness.

Officially Margaret now bore the title 'the Reverend Margaret Court'. But like anything that hinted of ostentation, she preferred to leave the title on her ordination certificate.

To avoid any accusation from either the wider church or the secular world that she was profiting personally from her ministry, especially as it grew in size and influence, she established it as an incorporated body. This put her personal wealth and assets, gained long before she ever thought of going into ministry, outside the financial side of the ministry. The ministry was to be strictly non-profit, giving to those who had little to give.

She gathered around her a ministry team of committed, mature Christians—twenty-six men and women from different denominations who gave voluntarily of their time and freely of their love. Each contributed their own particular gift to the ministry. 'I could not do it without them,' she readily admitted. God had shown her that she was to 'captain' this team by her own example, encouraging, guiding and teaching them the principles of leadership and responsibility. It was very similar to the days when she was captain of the Australian Federation Cup team and had taken the younger members under her wing. She had considered that appointment a great honour and felt no less honoured to be heading up God's team. And right from the start, she felt that she was to use her leadership skills to prepare her team to eventually go out into their own ministries. This would ensure that the labourers in God's harvest-field continued to increase, as they in turn trained up others the way she had trained them.

Margaret realised that the vision given to her by God had to be put into the hearts of her team if they were to fulfil the major aims of the ministry. In sport, a team can only play well if its members are united and have a shared understanding of their aims and the most effective way to achieve them. The ministry team already had an inherent unity because they were members of the same 'family'. Now she saw that imparting that vision to each team member would assure success, for a house united would surely stand.

The foremost aim and the core of the ministry's vision was to lead the lost, lonely and hurting to a personal and loving relationship with Jesus Christ. There was only one way that aim could be attained, Margaret stressed, and that was through love—the type of pure, unconditional love that Jesus said would never fail.

The ministry began to distribute gifts of food, finances, bedding and clothing to those in need, demonstrating God's love in a tangible way. All finances received were ploughed back into the ministry. The money was used to purchase the various items to be given away and to cover the inherent costs of ministry operations. Surplus funds were sown back into other mission work, both in Perth and overseas.

From the ministry's first public meeting in the Perth suburb of Kallaroo in March 1991, scores of people began to give their lives to Christ for the first time. Many others re-dedicated themselves to Christ after going through what can be best described as a 'wilderness' experience. Hundreds more were baptised in the Holy Spirit, with the evidence of speaking in a new tongue.

Defeated, depressed and downtrodden lives were constantly being changed in every meeting. Testimonies abounded, and none was more dramatic than that of Martin, who later told of his powerful conversion one night when Margaret taught on the love and character of God.

I was desperate. I really didn't know what I could do to salvage my marriage, which was in crisis. For a long time I'd hungered for the reality of God and had sought Him in many alternate ways and practices, but always I came up dry and empty. I became hard and hadn't cried for many years. In many ways I just went about my life, totally absorbed in my own selfish interests, ignoring my wife and family. But it all suddenly went wrong when I found that my wife was looking elsewhere for the love and affection that I wasn't giving to her.

I rang a Christian friend who suggested I go and hear Margaret Court speak. Although I wasn't a Christian, I was an avid squash player, and the thought of hearing Margaret Court was a real bonus. If she had no answers for me in what she preached, then at least I'd get to hear from the champion herself. But the minute she spoke, warm, powerful

waves came over me, and when an invitation was
given for people to come forward and be set free in
their lives by receiving Jesus I couldn't get to the
front quickly enough. I knew, I don't really know
how, that Jesus was the way, the truth and the life—
the answer to all those years of seeking. I knew I
needed Jesus to come into my life and transform me
into a better person.

As she prayed for me I couldn't help but cry.
Somehow it felt like my tears were ushering in a new
and better life, and at the same time washing away
the old life. My wife, who had agreed to come with
me in a final attempt to salvage our marriage, was
amazed at the sight of those tears. In all our twenty
years of marriage she had only ever seen me cry on
one occasion—the day my dog died!

Today our marriage is totally restored, better than
it was before. I truly believe my conversion to Chris-
tianity was nothing short of miraculous. That
meeting was my Damascus Road, and I will be eter-
nally grateful to Margaret for introducing me to
Jesus—the answer to all my problems.

There was not one dry eye in the hall on the night
when Jim stood to his feet and told his poignant story
of a young life, orphaned from the age of four, shat-
tered by abandonment, rejection and chronic child
abuse.

I trusted no one and hated everyone—especially
God, who had allowed such hurt and heartache in

my life under the hands of those who professed to be His servants. When I was old enough, if fifteen can be termed old enough, I turned to alcohol to numb the pain and anaesthetise me to the hurt of my lonely world. I hardened my heart and determined that nothing would ever again hurt me, and became very hostile and aggressive towards everything and everyone. It wasn't long before I went to prison for my aggressive behaviour. I had married, but of course that didn't last because I didn't know how to love anyone. In all my life I had never heard a single soul say the three most precious words, 'I love you', to me. For fifty years it was the same story.

Then one day Jim decided to go to a Margaret Court meeting—a day he would later describe as 'the best day in my whole life'. He had actually given up drinking at this stage, but he was still a very lost and lonely soul.

Margaret spoke about the love of God being able to heal all the hurts and rejections of the past if a person could forgive everyone who had hurt them. I was totally overwhelmed by the love and genuine warmth that seemed to flow from Margaret. She spoke as if she really knew God as a loving, heavenly Father, and I wanted that too. At the end of the meeting, she invited all those who had been hurt, wounded and bruised to go forward and receive prayer. I had to go forward because the love pulled me.

When Margaret prayed with me, I felt the love of God go right through my body and pierce my hardened heart. I willingly received Jesus Christ as my Lord and Saviour, right there and then, because I knew He had just healed my broken heart. Immediately, I knew that I'd be able to forgive all those who had ever hurt me and be free of the painful memories of the past. Margaret said that night that to be free to love and be loved, there had to be no areas of unforgiveness in our lives, regardless of the situation. 'Forgiveness will bring your healing,' she said, 'for as God has forgiven you of much, so you need to forgive others of much. Don't let unforgiveness get into your heart; give it all to God. He knows all about it and He alone is the avenger. Let it all go, for it will surely destroy you.'

In the weeks following that meeting, Jim searched out all those early educators and told them he had forgiven them. He also asked their forgiveness for his hatred towards them. He continued to come to the meetings and heard how he could start to use faith in his life to have his every need met. The night Jim gave his moving testimony, he ended by introducing his bride of just two months. 'For the first time I know how it feels to be really loved,' he said.

Jim went on to be happily married and attend a solid Christian church, his past life truly gone as he walked in the newness of life in Christ.

There were many other stories. Annie, a recent arrival from Britain, told of having many financial miracles happen in a short time after she attended a meeting where Margaret taught that every need, even financial, could be met by believing and acting on God's Word. Another lady told of how her headaches had totally disappeared as she sat and listened to Margaret teach the Word on healing. A woman with severe depression was healed in the same way. A young man who took a morning off work to attend a meeting was healed of a longstanding back ailment.

Margaret always emphasised that the glory for such wonderful changes in people's lives belonged to God. She realised that she could do nothing, and was nothing, without Him. Still, gratitude came to her from the people to whom she ministered. They knew it was her great love for them, and her willingness and obedience to bring them the gospel, that had been the turning point in their lives. For some that had meant the difference between life and death.

Others wrote letters to the ministry sharing their good news and declaring their heart-felt thanks. Here is one letter from a lady named Susan:

Dear Margaret and the ministry team,
During the last six months I began to feel unwell with symptoms that would come and go. I consulted my doctor who diagnosed a chemical imbalance in my body; this was due to the brain not regulating certain chemicals in my body properly. This imbalance was caused by a crash diet I went on twelve years previously for which I was hospitalised and given medical treatment. The only treatment my doctor could give me was drugs, which he felt reluctant to do because of my age.

During the month of July I went to a Margaret Court meeting. Margaret prayed for me and Jesus healed me! Since that night I have felt completely different. I now have plenty of energy; I feel whole and well on the inside.

I know Jesus is real and He does heal today. He heals physically, emotionally, mentally and spiritually. He knows everything there is to know about a person and each of their needs. He wants to make them free and whole. I know this is true because Jesus healed me.

Many people told similar stories of needs met through Margaret's ministry. But she, more than anyone, knew they needed to learn, as she had, the spiritual principles of why they received as they did and how it was all made possible through Jesus Christ. Each person who made a decision for Christ was encouraged to attend a local church which preached God's Word rather than religious traditions. Here, Margaret felt, the principles which often they had received but not fully understood could be learnt and expanded in a living, caring fellowship.

At the same time, the ministry provided an encouraging nucleus of strong, loving support and teaching for those who were not ready to stand alone. Over the next four years, this 'discipleship' work became possibly the greatest thrust of her ministry. She realised that many who received no further knowledge would perish, as she almost did, if the Word of God was not built into them. The counselling team worked hard to contact and visit all those who had urgent needs and required more support.

Nothing was done in Margaret's ministry without prayer to prepare the path ahead. Before each meeting, the ministry team would pray to break down barriers of resistance to the Word going forth, and to accomplish the salvation of all those who would be attending. The years Margaret spent heading intercessory prayer groups had seen her develop into a mighty prayer warrior who knew when, how and what to pray. Her spiritual antennae were finely tuned to the Holy Spirit.

Frequently, the people who received in the meetings were those whom she and her team had already prayed and believed God for—sometimes with tears. God often revealed those who were in pain or suffering from feelings of despair and hopelessness long before the actual meetings, so that the snares holding them in bondage would be broken and they would be free to receive in the meeting. Margaret emphasised that every single person was valuable and precious to God. She saw them with His heart of mercy, compassion and love. She listened caringly and with understanding, never judging, just giving out the wisdom of God from His Word that she knew would change any situation from defeat into victory.

Margaret developed a particular concern for families. She was truly saddened by family breakdown, whatever the relationship. Divorce to her was a type of cancer eating into the hearts of men, women and children. One of her ministry's principal goals was the desire to bring family groups back together in the unity of love and fellowship. She wanted to see the family unit restored and repaired through the love of Christ.

She taught that a nation is only as strong as its building blocks, and healthy societies are made up of strong family units. The family unit was under attack in Australia, as it was all over the world, especially through the breakdown of marriage. Over forty per cent of first-time marriages ended in divorce. Marrying a second or third time did nothing to reduce the percentage as such marriages failed quicker and at an even greater rate. She believed that pride and unforgiveness, the inability to say 'I'm sorry', was often the principal reason behind marriage breakdowns.

Margaret, like so many others, faced the possibility of a crisis in her own marriage in its early years because she didn't want to give in on any issue if she felt she was justified. Her stubborn streak was well known. She had only been married a short time when she had a disagreement with Barry. Not satisfied with the way the argument developed—or rather didn't develop, as Barry would not be drawn in—she withdrew into a shell of sulky silence, refusing to discuss the matter further. She busied herself and pretended not to notice Barry, secretly hoping he would ask her something and then she could ignore him. But Barry simply walked up to her and said in his abrupt, honest manner, 'Now, we'll have no more of that sort of behaviour around here. If you've got something to say, say it and get it off your chest.'

Nobody had ever brought her face-to-face with her moodiness so abruptly. Like most champion athletes, she was prone to mood swings almost without knowing it. They came with the stress, the nature and outcomes of competition, the inherent highs and lows that went with celebrating a win or lamenting a loss. Withdrawal had become a way of life for her as she learnt to focus totally on a game ahead. And she had always avoided publicity, being terribly fearful of public speaking. So she rarely learnt to voice her strongly-held opinions, choosing to keep them deep within.

Barry's direct statement took her by surprise, but she quickly saw that he had hit on the real crux of the matter. She had not liked the tension between them any more than he had, and immediately saw how childish her behaviour was in the light of his words. She apologised and resolved not to let anything stay in her heart against Barry and build into resentment. She loved him and she knew he loved her, and she saw that it was foolish to have hostile, unspoken words between them. From that point on their marriage grew strongly because she felt free to be open and honest with Barry, and there were rarely bad words between them. Forgiveness flowed freely; Margaret was always ready to say, 'I'm sorry, please forgive me,' as was Barry, who did not know how to hold a grudge.

Margaret and Barry had a firm belief in the sanctity and commitment of their marriage vows even before they became Christians. Christianity simply strengthened and confirmed their belief that marriage was ordained by God. Margaret saw her relationship with Barry as a physical bond, while her relationship with God was a spiritual bond. A good marriage combined the physical and the spiritual into a godly unit that no man could put asunder. Likewise, a strong Christian life combined the spiritual with the physical to ensure success in all areas of life.

Margaret believed strongly that such important commitments as marriage and accepting Christ should be done publicly before a crowd of witnesses. Marriage is an oath taken before witnesses, and accepting Jesus should also be done before witnesses. She felt that private commitments, like New Year's resolutions, soon lost their conviction. She had no time for those who were afraid to confess Jesus publicly with the excuse that religion was a private matter.

She saw other parallels between marriage and the Christian life. To have a truly successful marriage, each partner had to 'die' to self and esteem the other more highly than themselves. Likewise, to have a truly successful Christian life, a person needed to die to self so that Christ could truly live within. Then the union would surely live—this time eternally.

Margaret often shared these godly principles of marriage because inherent in them were the basics of the unity that she saw needed to come into the segmented and divided Body of Christ if the world was going to be won to Christ. In a far greater sense, death must come to all would-be servants of Jesus so the Body of Christ could rise and live and be greater than any single denomination or individual.

Every meeting of the ministry was unique as the Holy Spirit moved through Margaret in various ways to meet

people's varying needs. Common to them all was the
fact that Margaret operated under a powerful anointing
of the Holy Spirit. That anointing—the powerful, over-
whelming sensation of the presence of God—was not
always apparent, either to her or to those she ministered
to, for the Holy Spirit seemed always to be free to move
as He willed through her. But the reality of the anointing was seen by its effects, with many people falling
under the powerful presence of God, the Word and the
Holy Spirit residing within her.

The gifts of the Spirit were manifested in the meetings
because she had asked for them to flow and was obedient to let them flow. The gifts, she taught, were there
to allow people to receive from God what they needed.
Whether she was teaching the Word, laying hands on
the sick, prophesying, speaking forth an utterance in
tongues to be interpreted, or simply holding someone
in a loving embrace, God moved with power through
her sensitivity and obedience. God knows only too well
that everyone is different and will receive in a different
manner.

Not only did Margaret operate in the gifts of the
Spirit; so too did her team. She constantly told them to
desire the gifts to meet the needs of the people for which
they were designed.

The ministry Margaret developed at this time was not
unique. There were many others around the world who
emphasised the same truths and did so in a similar
manner, reaching out with an evangelistic thrust to the
poor. But a steady stream of love from Margaret and
the ministry team in all areas characterised this as a

ministry of love. In fact, many said the love was 'tangible'—that they felt it as they walked through the doors. People often testified that this was the reason they had surrendered their life to Christ: 'because for the first time in my life I felt really loved, wanted and accepted, just as I was'.

Margaret came to see this as the greatest compliment she and her team could be given. This was the love that motivated her originally to establish the ministry, and this was the love she desired to see continue its work in people's lives. It was the unconditional, self-sacrificing love that Jesus said would show people His true disciples—those doing the work of reconciling a defeated world to Him by showing the love of God that never fails.

CHAPTER 8

TRAINING AN ARMY

The Formation of Victory Life Centre

Margaret Court Ministries had held meetings for nearly five years when Margaret sensed they were to stop. There seemed to be a new direction to take. It was 1995 and the ministry was very successful in winning the lost to Jesus, but there were few churches where the new converts could be sent so others could disciple them. Since their first contact with the things of the Spirit had been with Margaret, many people followed her meetings around the city. They didn't want to go anywhere else.

Margaret wanted to work with the many churches in the city, feeding the new 'sheep' into existing 'flocks'. But she found so few that would nurture them in the ways of the Spirit and prayer and teach them the Word of faith.

She and a group of intercessors had prayed for years that God would raise up pastors in Perth who had a shepherd's heart for the sheep, as she had herself. But she never contemplated starting a church until God spoke to her. 'I want you to start the work which you are praying for Me to start in this city,' she sensed Him saying. 'You are the one. You are not the first. I have raised up others in this city, but they have not responded. So, because it is in your heart, I am going to raise you up as a voice to this city, and the nation, and the nations.'

This was no small matter, and Margaret sought as much confirmation as she could. If establishing a church was God's will for her, she felt she could do it. She zealously sought the Lord in prayer and asked Him for a scripture on which the church could be built. She was directed to the same scriptural foundation that underpinned the formation of Margaret Court Ministries half a decade before:

> Is this not the fast that I have chosen: to loose the bonds of wickedness, to undo the heavy burdens, to let the oppressed go free, and that you break every yoke? Is it not to share your bread with the hungry, and that you bring to your house the poor who are cast out; when you see the naked, that you cover him, and not hide yourself from your own flesh?
>
> Then your light shall break forth like the morning, your healing shall spring forth speedily, and your righteousness shall go before you; the glory of the Lord shall be your rear guard. Then you shall call, and the Lord will answer; you shall cry, and He will say, 'Here I am.'
>
> If you take away the yoke from your midst, the pointing of the finger, and speaking wickedness, if you extend your soul to the hungry and satisfy the afflicted soul, then your light shall dawn in the darkness, and your darkness shall be as the noonday. The

Lord will guide you continually, and satisfy your soul in drought, and strengthen your bones; you shall be like a watered garden, and like a spring of water, whose waters do not fail. Those from among you shall build the old waste places; you shall raise up the foundations of many generations; and you shall be called the Repairer of the Breach, the Restorer of Streets to Dwell In. (Isaiah 58:6–12)

The final go-ahead came one morning as God spoke to her while she was doing her breakfast dishes, looking out over the beautiful Swan River: 'I want you to start this work. Step out and I will show you how to do it as you go.' It was clear and it was definitely God. And so the decision was made.

Finding people to assist in establishing a church was not a problem. She had spent nearly five years training a group of people who had proven themselves loyal and faithful and were ready to step up to another level. She consulted with respected team members, family and friends. They all wholeheartedly encouraged her that she could do what God had asked.

The vision grew quickly. Margaret saw a church that would be like an army boot camp, where people from all walks of life could come and be formed into a strong fighting force for Jesus. She wanted this church to have a purpose—to train up an army of men and women who knew who they were in Christ and who could take the city and the nation for Jesus.

She saw a church that would be a centre of mercy, love and compassion. It would be like a 'mercy ship' to the city of Perth, providing refuge and shelter to those in need.

She saw a church that would be a centre of teaching, training and discipling others, providing many ways for people to receive from God's Spirit and grow strong in His Word.

She saw a church that would take in missionaries from other nations and equip them with all they would need to return and establish works of their own.

Margaret felt strongly about the naming of the church. It would be 'Victory Life Centre'. Each word had special significance for her.

'Jesus died to give every single person on this earth an abundant, victorious life, not one full of tragedy, defeat, sickness, sin and death,' she explained. 'He has already won the battle for us. He died so that we can live. We can live here on earth as it is in heaven, for Jesus has already won the battle for us to live in victory.'

She also wanted the name to reflect the joy, vibrancy and power that comes from living a life truly connected to the life in Jesus. 'We need the life of God in our lives, in our church, in our midst,' she said. 'If God is not involved in our services we simply have a man-made ritual and it becomes a lifeless and powerless religious ceremony. It's time to show the world that Jesus is alive because of the abundant life He lives through each and every one of us!'

Finally, the church needed to be a centre where people could come and find the help they needed. She illustrated her vision graphically using the image of a tree of life, with various works operating from its core—just as the life of a tree flows from the trunk out to the branches offering food, shelter, shade and rest (see diagram). It was here, from the central core, that she saw that the lost, the lonely, the poor, the needy and the physically and mentally sick could be given help to overcome.

For the first service in July 1995, Margaret rented an auditorium located in Homebase, an expo centre for furniture and building materials located in the Perth suburb of Wembley. That morning there were just under 100 people in attendance. High on the overhead projector went the vision she had for each area of the church in the shape of a tree. It went far beyond just having a Sunday morning or evening service. On that tree were branches showing the many parts of the vision she had conceived in her spirit.

Every branch represented a different 'department' with a different function. But they all had one goal: 'souls'. Margaret knew that often the lost, lonely, wounded and hurting need to feel and experience the love of God in action before they can really believe in Him. Everything in the church was to be done for that purpose.

Within the first few months the church experienced radical growth. Many were attracted because it was a church where ministry to the sick was a high priority. Sunday night services were always for the sick.

But there were those who needed more ministry than just one Sunday a week. 'Many people need an intensive care unit,' Margaret said. 'Without help, they will grow worse and depressed and perhaps not recover at all. Sickness, disease and depression do not attack just on Sundays but every day and night.'

So Margaret began a daily 'Healing School' where people could come and sit under the Word for four days a week and learn how to receive their healing. This intensive care treatment enabled their faith to grow to a point where they could appropriate the healing promises of God. Such faith takes time to develop, as one dose of God's Word will not dispel thirty or forty years of wrong teaching and misconception overnight.

Margaret took these services and gradually trained others in her team to also minister healing (the only qualification any believer needs to have a 'healing ministry' is to believe that all healing is done by the power of the Holy Spirit through the authority that is in the name of Jesus). Because some people were encouraged during the meetings but a few hours later felt fearful, agitated and alone again, Margaret started to handwrite sheets of scripture, and encouraged people to take these and get the audio tapes of the meetings so they could go over the healing Word again and again.

All those whose doctors said 'there is no hope' were the very ones Margaret wanted to tell 'there is always hope in Jesus'. The testimonies that came from these meetings were wonderful. Fran, for example, a woman from Terrigal in New South Wales, wrote:

I have been a Christian for forty years and was diagnosed with cancer four-and-a-half years ago. I had immediate surgery and an eight pound tumour was removed from my stomach. It was then that the specialist warned of my life span being no more than two to five years or even less!

About a year later another major surgery took away another larger tumour ... and I was warned that I would most likely need one more operation. I might add that there was no other form of treatment I could have, only surgery.

I have always had a strong faith in the power of our wonderful God and in the healing power of the Great Physician, the Lord Jesus Christ. This led me to attend a number of healing services, including the laying on of hands and anointing with oil at the hands of my minister, in accordance with the scripture in James 5:16.

Two years after my operation I was again in hospital for a third major surgery, and according to the medical profession the last that could be given me. I had a very hard time in hospital and spent a long time in recovery—two weeks longer than before. Four months later, another CT scan showed that I had a further tumour, the size of a 50 cent piece on the scan. Another scan needed to be taken in four months to check its growth.

Taking these matters into consideration, I was told to visit my daughter in Perth while I was still well enough to travel, for I would [soon] no longer be able to do so.

It was while I was in Perth in November 1995 that the Lord led me to enquire about Margaret Court's healing services. Our daughter, who was a Christian,

*had a friend who was a counsellor with Margaret
Court and she took me to the healing service.*

*At that service I went forward for prayer and did
not really notice if anything had taken place. Again
the Lord guided me to return the very next day.
Pastor Gloria [one of Margaret's co-workers] spoke
on the theme 'hope' and she gave her testimony. I
stood at the front with many others and finally came
away just knowing that my glorious Saviour had
healed me that very day. Praise God!*

*Three months later, my CT scan showed that I was
completely healed. That is nineteen months ago, and
four CT scans later there has been no sign of any
tumours. Isn't God in the power of His Son, the Lord
Jesus Christ, loving and powerful? While I am a little
restricted in my activities through the effects of the
surgery, I continue to thank God for allowing me to
witness and minister to many in similar circumstances that need the touch of His hand and the
assurance of His divine love.*

Another facet of Margaret's vision came into being
in February 1997, just eighteen months after the first
service of Victory Life Centre was held. It was a dream
come true as she cut the cord to display the sign for
'Victory Life Bible Training Centre', where students
would be taught the Word and how to apply it in their
lives. She wanted everyone to have an opportunity to
study the Bible in a professional manner but with a
practical emphasis.

'I want this to be a Training Centre where people can

come and hear how to live a full, complete and successful life by learning how to put the Word of God into their lives,' she told the sixty-four students of the Charter Class. 'This Bible Training Centre is for everyone—from the housewife to the professional, and especially for those called to the ministry. Daily classes will teach you how to walk in the Word that promises to bring you into victory, health and prosperity, fulfilment and contentment, all the days of your life.'

'I did two years of Bible School,' wrote one student later. 'I came in knowing absolutely nothing about the Bible or what it said. I had only recently given my heart to Jesus, and it was the best thing I ever did.'

And so it went with each facet of her vision. A children's department. A youth department. A large missions department, continuing the kind of work among the poor that was a feature of Margaret Court Ministries. Margaret wanted to have God's blueprint for every expansion of Victory Life Centre, so before each development there was the same earnest preparation. The work had to be built on the foundations of prayer, the Word and the Spirit.

The church was established in prayer long before any practical arrangements were made. 'We all need to seek the will, wisdom and counsel of God in all we do and say,' Margaret says. 'We have the Holy Spirit within us and we only need to press in and find out what He has already prepared for us to walk in. We see this principle in the Old Testament where God promised Israel that He had already prepared the land for them. They only had to walk into it and claim what was theirs. But stubbornness, rebellion, doubt, grumbling and division kept them out of that land. Instead of taking the eleven-day journey and doing what God said they were well able to do, they spent forty years and finally perished in the wilderness.

'Many churches will arise in these end times and do in one year what other churches have failed to do in forty years simply because they are open to the voice of God and are obedient to His will. We want to be a church that knows how to move with the cloud by day and rest by the pillar of fire by night.'

Strength and courage, power and provision, vision and godly direction only come from spending time in the presence of God in prayer. Margaret leads by example and prays for God's wisdom in every decision that needs to be made. This does not make her infallible, but accountable. She readily and humbly admits to mistakes and learns their painful lessons. Her constant prayer is to stay in the presence of God so that her spiritual ears are sensitive to hear and discern His voice saying, 'This is the way, walk in it'.

Then there is the Spirit. The Bible says, *'The letter kills, but the Spirit gives life'* (2 Corinthians 3:6). The invited presence of God in the person of the Holy Spirit is uppermost in all Victory Life Centre services.

'If God doesn't turn up then there's no point in us turning up,' she explains. 'The presence of God in our midst is an absolute necessity, and we are certainly not going to have any service without having God in attendance.

'I want to see the glory of God manifest in our midst.

It's our job to make sure that we provide God a suitable sanctuary through praise and worship and waiting on Him. Our meetings should never be so legalistic and ritualistic that God never gets an opportunity to minister His healing, deliverance and salvation to the people. We must stay open, always spiritually alert and sensitive to the voice of the Holy Spirit as He leads our services.

'If church services are not seeing people saved, healed, delivered and changed then it's obvious the Spirit of God is not moving. I never want to have a service so structured and organised that God Himself cannot fit into the program.'

For too long churches have used the idea that God is a God of order and decency to stifle the Holy Spirit, she believes. 'Breaking out into laughter or joy, weeping or laying prostrate on the ground are actions often condemned by those who say they cannot be of God. But we're not going to put God into a box. It's time to see God manifest in our services directing people to cry, weep, laugh, sing, run around the auditorium, dance or whatever! We've seen so many healings and miracles come when people have simply obeyed God and not the traditions of men.'

Third, there is the Word. Margaret does not preach any opinion or conviction that does not line up with the Word of God. 'In any situation we need to say what God says and not what the world, our feelings or anything else says,' she adamantly declares time and time again.

'There is truth in the world, but the Word of God is

the highest form of truth. If a person is dying of cancer, that can be the truth. But this cancer is subject to a higher truth—God's Word! The Word tells that a person can be healed of cancer by receiving the benefits of Jesus' substitutionary death on Calvary. Jesus died not just for sin, but also to free man from the price that sin exacts, which is sickness and premature death.

'Many people do not know that God's Word is pure and true. God's Word has within it creative power to alter every situation. Miracles are simply God's Word applied over natural circumstances.'

It is through the balanced operation of His Spirit and His Word that Jesus grows His church. 'If a church just has the Word it will eventually dry up. If a church just has the Spirit and manifestations of the Spirit it will eventually blow up. If a church has a balance of the Word and the Spirit it will develop and grow up. We must have both to remain totally balanced in every area.'

By the end of 1997 the crowds at Victory Life Centre had grown and the seating capacity was stretched to the limit. It was decided to relocate the church and take the pressure off the crowded children's and youth departments, at the same time moving the Training Centre, which was meeting elsewhere, into the same building.

A new location was found—the Tom Wilding Pavilion at the Claremont Showgrounds. With the lease came a stipulation that during the annual Show, the church would have to move out to make way for an exhibition of wild and exotic animals.

However, when Show time came, it was decided that rather than move out and then back after two weeks, it was time to buy a building. The finances were healthy, despite the recent expense of moving into the Showgrounds. A search ensued, with many people on the lookout for a building to enable growth and future development. All knew that Margaret's vision could not be contained within a normal sized building. A carpet warehouse situated right outside the city centre of Perth was located in Osborne Park. It was purchased for a good price and, for the third time, Victory Life Centre was on the move.

An auditorium was sculpted out of a run-down storage area. Soon it was equipped with new carpet, air conditioning, heating and a sound system. Offices were established, a lift installed and fire stairs built. The black and grimy walls welcomed a freshening coat of paint and the addition of curtains turned the old warehouse into a building that bore some resemblance to a church. Flowers and greenery added to the effect.

Services began there in July 1998. The building was officially dedicated and opened in December with a wonderful ceremony conducted jointly by former West Australian Premier Sir Charles Court and Rev. Dennis Burke from the USA.

Victory Life Centre continues to grow. It is now one of the largest churches in Perth, with nearly 800 people attending weekly. Every Sunday morning over 100 children, from babies through to twelve years of age, receive ministry from anointed leaders and pastors. The number of young people aged 13–25 is in the hundreds;

they have built a new-look youth ministry area called 'Brickyard' under the main auditorium, complete with their own Cafe. Skate ramps and basketball hoops are just the start of their vision for a large sporting complex in the years ahead.

Seeing Christian kids having fun is a great way to reach those outside Christ. Many young people are relieved to see that they don't have to surrender their personality at the door to become a 'Christian'. The church also now supports twenty affiliated churches and ministries across Australia and overseas. 'Victory Life International' was formed to be the central base from which these affiliated ministries could draw support, help and training while remaining completely autonomous. More and more churches are seeking the type of support that fledging works often need if they are to mature and become strong in themselves.

The Training Centre plays an increasingly important role. Right from its inception, Margaret has declared that people from all nations will come to it. Along with full-time, part-time and correspondence courses, the Centre hopes soon to step up teaching stations on the Internet.

The 'miracle ministry' of Victory Life Centre also continues stronger than ever, and there are plans underway to further enlarge it. Many terminally ill patients need treatment day and night. It disturbs Margaret to see people who could live die prematurely. All they need, she believes, is to be in a place where they can receive the Word around the clock, along with any needed medical treatment.

'I've always "seen" people coming from every nation to this place,' she says. 'They come and return healed. I see Christian doctors and nurses working alongside pastoral carers, all contributing to the total recovery of the patient. We will have the Word of God on tape day and night until that Word takes seed in them and drives the sickness right out of their bodies.'

Then there is the missions work. From the very beginning there has been an emphasis that feeding and clothing the poor must be a vital part of this church. A big missions department was established to handle the large numbers of people who come in seeking help every day. Over ninety food hampers are given out each week to poor and needy families. Large freezer units have been installed to cope with the amount of food that is coming through the Centre daily. Clothing and furniture are also gratefully received by those who come into the church in great need.

The long-awaited evangelistic thrust of the church is also starting to appear on the wings of its outstanding missions projects. There's nothing like telling people how good God is when they are able to come and have their practical needs met in an atmosphere of love and acceptance. Many people come to know Christ through this arm of the church and are then ushered into courses suitable for their needs.

Ahead is a vision of a sprawling campus where each department—children, youth, music, theatre arts and drama, audio visuals, missions outreach—will be housed comfortably in its own area running its own programs. There are plans to have three buses and everything needed to hold outreaches in the city and the market places. A major sporting complex is also planned where the facilities can be changed into auditoriums for mass rallies. There are many prominent sportsmen and women in the church, and Margaret sees a need for Christians in sport to be encouraged to become powerful ambassadors for Christ.

Few of the businesses around the church realise that there is a large group of intercessors praying for their success and prosperity so that their current premises will soon have to be vacated to make way for Victory Life Centre's future growth. By faith the church has already claimed and named the whole street 'Victory Life Boulevard'!

That she is a woman in ministry—once a totally male-orientated domain—is not even a factor in Margaret's thinking. There are those who still question the idea of a woman taking such a prominent leadership role in the church. But Margaret knows she has been called by God and does not see her gender as an issue.

'Throughout my tennis career I always trained and practised with men. Never once did I feel inferior, unworthy or out of place with them. I was equal to them—not in a physical sense but in the sense of fulfilling my destiny right alongside them fulfilling theirs. I never once thought, "I'm a woman and they're men". We were all athletes. They never thought of me as inferior to them; they simply respected the gift and talent in me. This qualification should apply to ministry today. We are pastors, we are teachers, we are evangelists or whatever God has called each of us to be.'

She believes that God is about to release women into their true positions in the Body of Christ—a move that will restore to the Body a wonderful sense of unity and completeness. 'This is the sort of unity we see in blessed marriages. This is the sort of unity and oneness that the church lacks. It has long denied woman the role which God has purposed she fulfil in Him. The early church demonstrated this type of power in unity with mighty men and women labouring together to fulfil the Great Commission. The issue should never be whether a person is male or female but whether they are called and anointed of God.'

Margaret feels there has been an overreaction by both men and women to the word 'submissive' and a misunderstanding of the role of women in the home as opposed to their role in the church. The two are not the same. Biblical submission is the way that God provides protection for the woman (not abuse). Accordingly, the man should be the head, or authority, in the home as he provides, guards, protects, nurtures and loves his wife and family. His love for her will protect her from him making decisions that will in any way lord it over her. In this way he also gives his children a heritage of which they can be proud, for it has been said that there is no greater gift a man can give his children than to love their mother. Spiritually mature women have no problem with this divine order God implemented in the family unit.

'Everything in our lives will function well if we keep our priorities as God, then our husband, children, home, work and then ministry,' Margaret shared at a special mixed breakfast function for husbands and wives in November 1999. 'I praise God for my husband Barry, who is secure and strong within himself and is not threatened by anything I do which seems to put him in an "inferior" position. He is head of the Pastoralists' and Graziers' Association of Western Australia, which is an important leadership position. When I was playing tennis he always encouraged and believed in me. When I became very sick from a torn heart valve he stood by me. And when I was called into ministry he encouraged me. I love to have my husband as the strength in my home, and when a decision needs to be made I trust him to make the right one where our family is concerned. It is never a dominant position of abuse but a respect we have for each other, and on most occasions we share and discuss views.'

For centuries churches have been full of women, a fact which shows their deep passion for the things of God. That is what makes women such wonderful intercessors. But it is time for the role of prayer warrior to lose its gender bias and become a work that both men and women can function in freely. More men need to become prayer warriors and intercessors, and more women need to step up into the positions to which God has called them.

'I guess I have always been one to accept a challenge in life. In tennis I was not afraid to head for unchartered waters. Where no woman had ever trained in a men's gym—I became the first. Where no woman had ever trained with weights—I did. Where no woman had ever come back after having a child to play professionally—

I did. Where no woman had ever taken her husband and children on tour with her—I did.

'And now looking back on my five years in ministry I see that starting this church has been another opportunity for me to take on a challenge of a totally different dimension. At times I've been tempted to quit, but not for very long! At times I've been hurt and disappointed in people, but not for very long! At times it has been hard, but it has also been very rewarding.'

And she never stops. Margaret Court Ministries has not been operational since 1995 due to Margaret's lack of time, but she sees it beginning to operate again as she is relieved of ministerial duties in other areas. She envisages the formation of a group of women as 'Women of Faith' to support each other and hold meetings and seminars around Australia. In the future she sees large healing meetings being held in the Perth Entertainment Centre, with lines of ambulances outside and people lining up with all sorts of stretcher-bound and wheelchair-bound cases, waiting by the thousands to get inside where they finally find God's healing and leave praising Him for His goodness.

Victory Life Centre is a living testimony to Margaret Court's tenacity, grit and determination. Already in five short years the things she saw in her spirit have come to pass, with more to follow. None of her team can afford to sit back and relax, even when they have forged ahead and achieved their immediate aims. It's like winning Wimbledon one day and getting back on the practice court the next!

CHAPTER 9

THE GREATEST MATCH OF ALL

One Sunday morning in July 1999, Margaret was standing in the pulpit at Victory Life Centre when there was a commotion at the side of the auditorium. She looked up as 600-plus people began cheering and Channel 9's Mike Munro, followed by a television camera, walked across and declared to her astonishment, 'Margaret Court, this is your life!'

Later, in the glare of TV studio lights, family, friends, relatives, past tennis greats and members of her congregation gathered to tape a celebration of her great sporting and ministry achievements for Channel 9's popular show *This Is Your Life*.

In some ways it was a re-run of a similar event seven years earlier. In July 1992 Margaret celebrated her fiftieth birthday and a testimonial night was given in her honour. At that event too guests came from three different groups: her tennis partners and coaches, her ministry and church associates, and the members of her family. Many only knew one side of her life, but there were those, like Barry and her friends Anne and Helen, who were involved in all three aspects.

At both events people spoke about her never-say-die attitude, her trustworthiness, and her loyalty and value as a true friend. The sporting fraternity in particular pointed out her stubborn determination to perfect any task she undertook. Former practice players and coaches noted the fact that she worked harder and longer than any other individual they had ever known to get to the top in tennis. But the comments made in 1992 by those who knew her best—her own children—best describe the type of person she was then and still is today.

Lisa, her youngest daughter, then aged twelve, told the large crowd that her mother had always been there for her whenever she had needed her. Her mum had never let her down.

That reliability is characteristic of Margaret. Not only has she always been there for Lisa and other family members; she is there for anybody who needs her to be a friend, helper or counsellor. Her home, adjacent to the magnificent Swan River, had long been a proverbial oasis for those who found themselves buffeted by the inevitable storms of life. Indeed, it was the sheer number of people who sought her help that prompted her first moves into public ministry because she did not want her home to be too disrupted by the continual influx of visitors.

Back then, the people who came with their problems never left her home disappointed. She always seemed to be able to give a 'word in season', the Word they desperately needed to hear at that moment. She had a seemingly bottomless reservoir of God's Word within her.

And so it is today. 'The Word always works,' she encourages people, knowing that the scriptures she gives will often cut through to the root of a problem far quicker than any long, sympathetic discussions or detailed analysis. 'Always speak the desired answer, not the problem,' she counsels.

Her second youngest child, Teresa, then fifteen, spoke of how her mother did all the chores that no one saw or truly appreciated. And indeed, Margaret is an ordinary wife and mother, with the same family-related responsibilities as anybody else. Back in 1992, she often related in her meetings how she had cooked the family breakfast, made the beds, put out the washing and driven her children to school just hours before coming to minister. Her three girls still reside at home, while Daniel is manager of the family farm in Moora, 150 kilometres north of Perth.

Margaret is keen for people to see that she is not a spiritual 'guru', too heavenly minded to be any earthly good. For years during school holiday periods she could be found at the family property cooking huge amounts of food for shearing teams, something she still likes to do as time permits. She knows all about the pressures of raising a family and living in today's world. She is not removed from the realities of life—and believes no minister of Christ should be. But into all of the mundane chores and endless daily tasks she brings Christ.

'I don't separate my life into the sacred and the secular. Every day and every task can be totally rewarding if it is always done with the right heart motive of love. I can talk to God as freely when I am doing the ironing as when I go to be alone with Him in my study. God does not want me to be someone different when I'm with Him than I am all the time.'

Marika, Margaret's eldest daughter, then eighteen, commented that although they were a family of six, more often than not they had ten or more for dinner! This highlighted the generous side of her mother, who always shared everything and made everyone feel welcome in her home. Nearly a decade later she is still going strong, a great cook and organiser for many large family and church functions.

Margaret has no qualms about enjoying an obviously comfortable existence. 'Having material possessions isn't the problem,' she says. 'It's the love of things that is the real problem. The more you have, the more you can give away.' And indeed, she lives by this sound biblical principle, believing that God prospers His people so they in turn can help others less fortunate than themselves. Barry has the same generous nature, willing to share with or assist anyone, anytime.

When Daniel, Margaret's only son and eldest child, then twenty, unashamedly stood and told his mother that he loved her, few people in the audience remained unmoved. His statement was the legacy of Margaret's emphatic attitude that her ministry began in her home and worked its way outward to the public. Still today she does not act differently away from home than when she's there. She does not wear a ministry mask of 'holiness' to hide areas of impropriety in her personal life. She is careful to treat her own family well and not subject them to any outbursts of anger, selfishness or the neglect that familiarity often breeds.

She is acutely aware there is no alternative to walking in love at all times. And she always taught her family to ask for forgiveness if strife broke out. 'It doesn't matter who is right or who is wrong. Be quick to say you're sorry for your part,' she still teaches, for she knows that this 'clearing the air' of unforgiveness is vital in creating loving, strong relationships. True love is being able to forgive, time and time again.

This Is Your Life was eventually screened in September 1999, and for the rest of that year Margaret seemed to reap more and more honours. They came not only for her legendary sporting feats but also for her ministerial service to the general community. In October she was honoured in Sydney by Rev. Fred Nile as the Australian Citizen of the Decade. Then she and her family flew to Vienna in November where she joined the world's sporting greats as one of the nominees for the title of 'Sportswoman of the Century'.

But perhaps the most heartfelt praise came in January 2000 from a man she greatly respects, Rev. Richard Roberts of the United States.

Roberts, the President of Oral Roberts University in Tulsa, Oklahoma, was Margaret's guest speaker for the annual Victory Life International Convention. During the convention he revealed the reason why a man who cannot afford time away from his daily television healing program and the administration of the university had flown half way around the world to Perth.

'I want you all to know that Victory Life Centre is known all over Tulsa as the work that God has raised up in Western Australia,' he told the congregation on the final Sunday morning of the convention. 'I first saw this woman sitting in the congregation of a pastor's convention in the USA, and I thought, "Why, that woman looks like Margaret Court". Imagine my surprise when I was told that it was her. I knew she was a Christian, but I had no idea she had her own church and was a pastor who had come to that conference.

'When she came forward to receive prayer from me, the Holy Spirit told me that she was going to ask me to come to Perth and when she did I was to go. I said nothing to her. Two months later she wrote to me and asked if I would come to Perth, and of course I said yes. She knew nothing about what the Lord had spoken to me—I did not say anything to her until she asked me to come.

'I came because God told me to come, but I also came because I saw the heart of this woman. I do not leave Tulsa very often due to my schedule, but this is one place I know God has instructed me to come, and to inject both time and finances into the mighty work that is being done here.

'I know that God's hand is on this church. It will expand and grow and you will see great things happen here.'

Margaret has never sought publicity for herself and perhaps that is why it is coming so fast and furious now. She will go anywhere and do anything to bring glory to her Lord, as long as she is convinced God wants her to go.

Margaret Court is not a manufactured personality. She is as you find her: a friendly, statuesque woman with a great love for people, reflecting her great love for God. She considers herself an ordinary wife and mother, although she may be justified in esteeming herself more highly in the light of her tremendous tennis achievements. She portrays no sign of an inflated ego, just a healthy self-esteem based on who and what she is in Christ.

She always saw her tennis ability as a gift from God, one that many other people were also given but did not develop as she did. She coupled that great natural talent with a fierce determination to put her name into the world's record books. It's amazing to consider that no other tennis player, woman or man, has ever equalled her record of twenty-four Grand Slam singles titles, and probably never will. It's a most impressive way to be immortalised in tennis history.

She herself never exalts the achievement of any person who is naturally gifted. It is the endeavour they exhibit in developing their talent that meets with her approval. She always found it hard to be treated as someone special just because she could play tennis well. It was something she was good at and wanted to do. It didn't make her a better person, nor did it qualify her to speak as an authority on issues of magnitude, as sports stars today are often asked to do.

Tennis influenced her exterior world, but it never

changed her on the inside as a person. In her heart she felt there was something missing. It didn't matter that she was successful, famous and reasonably wealthy; that 'something' was always missing until she met Jesus Christ. Jesus made all the difference. She knows that it is only Jesus who can change the nature of the heart.

This is the message she is taking to the city of Perth, and ultimately to her nation, Australia. This is the message that will change and transform lives as it did hers. This is the message that will bring temporal victory and eternal salvation. This is the message that God has committed to her, and others like her, to take to the nations.

A life of example and a ministry of love and excellence are the priorities that dominate her life. She desires to do everything she does to the best of her ability, to develop her God-given talents to their fullest. She desires to cultivate a true shepherd's heart for the sheep of the flock and to search out all those who are without the True Shepherd. Her sole motivation is to serve God by showing her love to a world full of people who are in desperate need of the answers that can only be found by accepting Christ as the Lord and Saviour of their lives.

Margaret is no longer focused on competitiveness; those days are long behind her. She sees Victory Life Centre and her ministry as one part of the Body of Christ, fulfilling its role so that the entire Body can function as a whole. This is the type of unity that she prays will come in the world-wide Body, for it is the unity that Christ said would characterise His church in the last days. She believes that denominational walls are barriers to true unity and must come down for an unhindered flow of the Holy Spirit. As they come down, so will the echelons of lifeless religion, and each person will be able to do their part in reconciling the world to Jesus.

With Margaret there's no room for complacency or inactivity of any kind. Where others can see just one building, she has her eyes set on the whole street. Where others see a suburb, she sees a city. Where others see hundreds, she sees thousands. She is an apostle and she is a visionary. She is determined to press on with all the spiritual athleticism of a champion of God, playing the greatest match of all.

The chapters of Margaret Court's life are far from completed. The book of her life handed to her by Mike Munro in July 1999 is already out of date. There are many pages still to come as this extraordinary woman continues to break barriers, set new goals and finish the work to which she has been called.

THE PRAYER OF SALVATION

I was number one in the world in tennis. I had money and fame. But there was still something missing in my life. For thirty years I sat in a church pew, but no one ever told me that I needed to make a decision to ask Jesus Christ into my life as my own personal Saviour and Lord.

The Bible clearly states in Romans 10:9–10: *'If you confess with your mouth the Lord Jesus and believe in your heart that God has raised Him from the dead, you will be saved. For with the heart one believes unto righteousness, and with the mouth confession is made unto salvation.'*

By praying the following prayer, out loud, and believing it in your heart, you will have the same assurance of eternal life that I have today.

'Heavenly Father, I believe Jesus is Your Son and that You have raised Him from the dead. I thank You that You have forgiven and forgotten all my past mistakes—that old things have passed away and all things are now new. I am now born again. I have new life right from this moment. I have eternal life now in the name of Jesus and I thank You for it. Amen.' (2 Corinthians 5:17)

Congratulations and welcome to the family of God! I urge you to join a Word-based church to grow in the things of God. Please write and tell us of this wonderful decision you have made today.

Victory Life Centre
PO Box 20
Osborne Park WA 6917
Australia
Ph: +618-9201-1266. Fax: +618-9201-1299
E-mail: mcourt@victorylifecentre.com.au
www.victorylifecentre.com.au

I pray God's peace and protection on you and your family, and pray for success in everything you purpose to do in life.

Margaret Court